A PATTERN APPROACH TO INTERACTION DESIGN

Jan Borchers
Stanford University, USA

JOHN WILEY & SONS, LTD
Chichester • Weinheim • New York • Brisbane • Singapore • Toronto

Copyright © 2001   by John Wiley & Sons Ltd
               Baffins Lane, Chichester,
               West Sussex, PO19 1UD, England

               National 01243 779777
               International (+44) 1243 779777

e-mail (for orders and customer service enquiries): cs-books@wiley.co.uk

Visit our Home Page on http://www.wiley.co.uk
                        or
                 http://www.wiley.com

Other Wiley Editorial Offices

John Wiley & Sons, Inc., 605 Third Avenue,
New York, NY 10158-0012, USA

Wiley-VCH Verlag GmbH
Pappelallee 3, D-69469 Weinheim, Germany

John Wiley & Sons (Australia) Ltd, 33 Park Road, Milton,
Queensland 4064, Australia

John Wiley & Sons (Canada) Ltd, 22 Worcester Road
Rexdale, Ontario, M9W 1L1, Canada

John Wiley & Sons (Asia) Pte Ltd, 2 Clementi Loop #02-01,
Jin Xing Distripark, Singapore 129809

Library of Congress Cataloging-in-Publication Data

Borchers, Jan
   A pattern approach to interactive design / Jan Borchers
      p. cm. (Wiley series in software design patterns)
   Includes bibliographical references and index.
   ISBN 0 471 49828 9
      1. Human-computer interaction. 2. Computer software – Development. I. Title II.
   Series

   QA76.9. H85 B67 2001
   004'. 01'9–dc21   00-054570

British Library Cataloguing in Publication Data

A catalogue record for this book is available from the British Library

ISBN 0 471 49828 9

Typeset in Palatino by the author using LaTeX software
Printed and bound in Great Britain by Biddles Ltd, Guildford and King's Lynn.
This book is printed on acid-free paper responsibly manufactured from sustainable forestry,
for which at least two trees are planted for each one used for paper production.

The WILEY SERIES IN SOFTWARE DESIGN PATTERNS is designed to meet the needs of today's software architects developers, programmers, and managers interested in design patterns. Frank Buschmann, the Series Editor, as well as authors, shepherds, and reviewers will work collaboratively within the patterns community to strive for high-quality, highly-researched, thoroughly validated, classic Works which document accepted and acknowledged design experience. Priority will be given to those titles that catalog software patterns and pattern languages with a practical, applied approach in domains such as:

- distributed systems
- real time systems
- database
- business information systems
- telecommunications
- organizations
- concurrency
- networking

Books in the series will also cover conceptual areas of how to apply patterns, pattern language developments and architectural/component-based approaches to pattern-led software development.

TITLES PUBLISHED

- **PATTERN-ORIENTED SOFTWARE ARCHITECTURE, Volume 1**

Frank Buschmann, Regine Meunier, Hans Rohnert, Peter Sommerlad and Michael Stal

0 471 95869 7   476pp   1996   Hardback

- **PATTERN-ORIENTED SOFTWARE ARCHITECTURE, Volume 2**

Douglas Schmidt, Michael Stal, Hans Rohnert and Frank Buschmann

0 471 60695 2   636pp   2000   Hardback

- **A PATTERN APPROACH TO INTERACTION DESIGN**

Jan Borchers

0 471 49828 9   250pp   2001   Hardback

A PATTERN APPROACH TO INTERACTION DESIGN

Contents

Preface

Designing successful interactive systems requires user interface designers to work together with software engineers and application domain experts in an interdisciplinary team. A major problem within such groups is communication between team members. *Pattern languages* have been communicating design knowledge successfully within architecture and software engineering in the past. This book summarizes the state of pattern languages in human–computer interaction (HCI), and proposes a new pattern-based framework for interactive systems design. It extends the pattern idea to a uniform model for expressing design issues of HCI, software engineering, and application domain of a project.

As an example, the framework is applied to describe design issues for interactive exhibits and similar public "kiosk" systems. The patterns were drawn from the author's design experience from a number of such systems, starting with the *WorldBeat* project, in which an award-winning interactive music exhibit was developed. *WorldBeat* lets users interact with musical concepts in entirely new ways, from playing virtual drums, to finding tunes by humming, to improvising to a blues band without playing incorrectly, using just a pair of infrared batons. The patterns were then used and refined in the design of subsequent interactive exhibits, including the *Interactive Fugue* about classical music, the *Personal Orchestra* system to virtually conduct the Vienna Philharmonic, and the *Virtual Vienna* 3-D city tour.

The result is a comprehensive pattern language about user interface design for interactive exhibits and public systems. Also shown is the pattern language describing concepts of the application domain "music" in the original *WorldBeat* system, and several patterns of successful software engineering solutions in those systems. Finally, the design of a software tool to work with pattern languages is presented.

It is shown how the pattern-based framework improves communication within design teams, and helps creating a design rationale and corporate memory of design experience for follow-up projects, new team members, and teaching.

For updates to this book, and current information about HCI Design Patterns, please visit the HCI Patterns Home Page at http://www.hcipatterns.org/.

Series Foreword

Patterns have taken the software community by storm. Software developers have been enthusiastic about patterns ever since the seminal work *Design Patterns: Elements of Reusable Object-Oriented Software* by the *Gang of Four*. Since then, many books on sofware patterns have been published, most notably the *Pattern Languages of Program Design* (PLoPD) series featuring edited collections of papers from various software pattern conferences, and the *Pattern-Oriented Sofware Architecture* series with its many general-purpose, concurrency and networking patterns.

This book is not, however, "yet another pattern book". Rather it differs from the available pattern literature significantly and in many ways. It is thus unique as well as very valuable for anybody interested in learning about and using patterns.

The most significant difference from other software pattern books is its very subject. Jan is an expert in human–computer interaction (HCI). He has an immense knowledge in designing many different types of interactive systems, such as information kiosks and systems used as interactive exhibits. A quick check reveals that only few patterns for human–computer interaction are documented in contemporary pattern literature. *A Pattern Approach To Interaction Design* thus fills a blank spot in the software pattern space. It also offers a framework to use HCI, software engineering, and even application domain patterns together within a software project.

Another difference is that most human–computer interaction patterns available today deal with the "technical" design of various types of user interfaces, such as the design of forms in form-based interfaces, and techniques for flashing back erroneous user input to an interface. This book, in contrast, takes the user's view: it presents patterns that help to design user-friendly human–computer interfaces.

Moreover, Jan's HCI patterns do not specify how to arrange particular types of components, classes, or objects in a software system in order to ultimately arrive at a user-friendly system interface. Instead, his patterns help shape environments in which users are invited—and then feel well and safe—to use an interactive system.

1

This perspective is rarely considered in systems development. Whilst much effort is put into supporting developers in designing and implementing software systems— including, but not limited to, developer-centric patterns such as those from the *Gang of Four*—it is actually the end users who ultimately (must) live and work with the interactive software systems that developers build. Thus they need systems that are easy to use, as well as powerful and adaptable to their personal needs. Users want systems that support rather than hinder them in doing their job. Ideally, users need not even be aware of the fact that they are working and communicating with complex hardware and software technology.

The patterns in this book address these needs. For example, the patterns INVISIBLE HARDWARE and DOMAIN-APPROPRIATE DEVICES tell designers why it is important to hide complex and unfamiliar hardware technologies from the users of a system, and instead allow them to communicate with that system using devices and 'abstractions' they know from their domain. Other patterns, such as FLAT AND NARROW TREE and INFORMATION JUST IN TIME, deal with finding the fine balance between not swamping a user with too much information, and leaving him unguided by providing almost no information, or not the right kind.

All patterns are also presented so that end-users can understand and use them. These patterns enable them to talk to developers about what they expect from a human–computer interface. In addition, the patterns are interwoven into a pattern language. This provides users with a structured and defined process to actually apply these patterns: users can specify the human–computer interface that they like and want from a particular software system. In short, the pattern language in this book gives users a voice that allows them to communicate their needs to developers, and to actively participate in the development of a concrete system.

This is unique for software patterns, and it leads me to another key difference I found between Jan's and other software patterns: the focus on user needs, user participation, and shaping environments in which humans feel comfortable closely resembles Christopher Alexander's approach. They have less in common with the vast majority of software patterns, which typically follow engineering-oriented pattern approaches à la *Gang of Four*. Alexander's vision of patterns is that they should enable people to be able to actively shape the environments in which they live, step by step, so that they can feel at ease in these environments. At least they should be able to influence the construction and modification of their environments. In other words, the intention of Alexander's patterns is to shift power from master planners and architects to the many people who live and work in our world, so that their needs can be articulated and considered when building towns and houses. You cannot say analogous things about software patterns. Simply using Alexander's pattern form is not enough by far to claim that a pattern is "Alexandrian".

As you can see, there are a lot of things to explore in this book, and also to learn: new patterns as well as a new perspective on software patterns. And after reading so much "useful stuff", enjoy the little pattern language about the secrets of composing and performing blues music: it is included because it describes the application domain of the *WorldBeat* interactive music system, which is the running example for many of the other patterns in this book. Therefore I would like to invite you to share the new insights and "aha" effects that I got when reading this book.

Frank Buschmann
Siemens AG, Corporate Technology

Acknowledgements

This book developed out of my work at the University of Linz in Austria, and at the Universities of Darmstadt and Ulm in Germany. I would not have succeeded without the help of many people, especially those mentioned below to whom I would like to express my gratitude:

Max Mühlhäuser from the University of Darmstadt supported this work in countless ways, and his ideas and comments contributed significantly to its success. Michael Weber from the University of Ulm in Germany offered me a place to work at as visiting scientist and lecturer, and Hans-Jürgen Hoffmann from the University of Darmstadt gave me valuable feedback on drafts of this work.

My colleagues at Linz, Ulm, and Darmstadt were responsible for that atmosphere of creative exchange necessary for such a project to evolve, and helped me with countless practical issues. Many students, in particular Günter Obiltschnig, Harald Hattinger, Rainer Gutkas, Wolfgang Samminger, Jörg Lehner, Werner Stadler, and Thomas Hellwagner at Linz, as well as Matthias Dannenberg and Ingo Grüll at Ulm, contributed to the practical side of this work through Master's theses and software projects, and often worked extra hours on implementations.

Many international colleagues gave valuable comments on the ideas underlying this work, at conferences, workshops, and in online discussions. I would especially like to thank Jim Coplien for his remarks about Alexander's ideas, Austin Henderson for his radical views on pattern-based software, Richard Griffiths and Lyn Pemberton for co-organizing all those HCI pattern workshops, and Tom Erickson for his valuable feedback on an early draft of this text. Finally, Gaynor Redvers-Mutton and her colleagues at Wiley were an excellent and helpful team to work with during the editing process.

But above all, my parents enabled me to take this path, and my wife Annette showed patience and understanding, despite my constant travel and work demands, and her own research work.

Jan Borchers
Stanford, February 2001

Chapter 1

Introduction

"Press Ctrl + Alt + Delete to log on."

—Microsoft Windows NT® opening screen.

1.1   Why User Interfaces Matter

Human–Computer Interaction, or HCI, deals with the interface between people and computer systems:

HCI: Human–Computer Interaction

> "In human–computer interaction knowledge of the capabilities and limitations of the human operator is used for the design of systems, software, tasks, tools, environments, and organizations. The purpose is generally to improve productivity while providing a safe, comfortable and satisfying experience for the operator."
> [Helander et al., 1997, p. xi]

A working group of the Special Interest Group for Computer-Human Interaction (SIGCHI) of the Association for Computing Machinery (ACM) has published recommendations for a human–computer interaction curriculum [ACM SIGCHI, 1992]. Fig. 1.1 shows their graphical

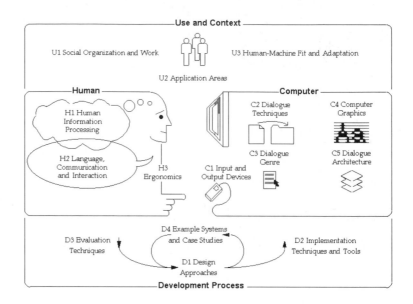

Figure 1.1: The ACM SIGCHI HCI Design Curriculum [ACM SIGCHI, 1992].

overview of the field, which conveys an idea of the scope of HCI in research and practice.

Importance of good user interface

There are numerous reasons why the quality of a user interface is critical to the success of an interactive system [Shneiderman, 1998, pp. 16 ff.]:

- life-critical systems require rapid and error-free performance of the operator;

- office, home and entertainment applications require ease of learning, low error rates, and subjective satisfaction to compete in the marketplace;

- new exploratory, creative, and cooperative systems need to fulfil high user expectations, ideally by having the computer vanish;

- systems need to accommodate human diversity in terms of physical, cognitive, and perceptual abilities, cultural and personality differences, especially catering for elderly or disabled users.

Moreover, there is a strong business case for human factors: Attention to those factors, and a careful, iterative design of the user interface of a system, can reduce development time and cost, the need for updates, and improve the success of the product in the market [Klemmer, 1989, Chapanis, 1991, Landauer, 1995]. With the advent of the World-Wide Web, e-commerce, public information terminals and similar systems, the number of first-time, one-time users increases, which makes careful user interface design even more critical to the success of such systems. For example, IBM recently gained a 400% increase in online sales (and an 84% decrease in help button usage) after redesigning their web site according to usability principles [Tedeschi, 1999].

Business case for human factors

IBM usability study

Creating the user interface portion of an interactive system is no minor task. A survey by Myers and Rosson [1992] reported that, on the average, 45% of the design and 50% of the implementation time for interactive applications were devoted to their user interface.

User interface: about 50% of design and implementation

1.2   Interdisciplinary Design and Its Problems

It should be obvious that successful design of an interactive system requires people from various disciplines to work together in a team.

Interdisciplinary design is necessary

> "GUIDELINE: The most successful designs result from a team approach where people with differing backgrounds and strengths are equally empowered to affect the final design."
> [Tognazzini, 1992, p. 57]

Key disciplines in this respect are software engineering, human interface design, and the application domain in which the system is going to be used. Other disciplines regularly involved include marketing, technical writing, graphic design, and others.

High return on
investment in UI
designers

A study by Jeffries et al. [1991] showed that human interface designers delivered the highest return on investment of any member in a software team, finding three to four times more problems in a software package within the same or shorter time than simultaneously conducted user tests, software engineers checking guidelines, and software engineers doing a cognitive walkthrough of the design.

User-centred design

To ensure that an interactive system solves problems that the intended users actually have, and that its interface uses the native terminology and concepts of the application domain, the design team must identify the prospective users and become familiar with their activities [Newman and Lamming, 1995, p. 91]. This "user-centred" approach to design [Norman and Draper, 1986] may involve consultation of experts of the application domain, or actual prospective users, to acquire this knowledge. This user involvement is usually essentially a one-way communication in which the designers extract information from users by means of surveys, questionnaires, interviews, and user tests.

Participatory design

A more active participation of users throughout the design process is suggested by the school of *participatory design*. There is no single, encompassing definition of this approach, but its central goal is that "... the ultimate users of the software make effective contributions that reflect their own perspectives and needs, somewhere in the design and development lifecycle of the software." [Muller et al., 1997, p. 258]. This recent article also gives an excellent overview of participatory design practice; for a more detailed treatment of the subject, see, for example, Schuler and Namioka [1997].

Interdisciplinary
communication is
difficult

A major problem of interdisciplinary design is effective communication. Users do not understand the technical jargon of software engineers or human factors people. Similarly, the design professionals initially usually have only a vague knowledge of the concepts, methods, and terminology of the application domain, and they have difficulties understanding them when users explain these issues to them.

As Kim [1990] points out, disciplines are like cultures: to work together, they must learn to appreciate one another's language, traditions, and values. However, people within a discipline often have trouble communicating what they know to outsiders. This is especially problematic for user interface, design because to succeed, it requires many disciplines to cooperate as outlined above: HCI needs to communicate.

If this communication fails, the result is that the methods, paradigms, and ultimately the values of each profession are not understood, and consequently cannot be respected, by the other disciplines. Any method that simplifies this mutual understanding would benefit the design process, and the resulting product.

1.3 Capturing Experience

Another important goal of any design team is to capture the reasons for design decisions, and the experience from past projects, to create a *corporate memory* of design knowledge.

Such a repository can have many benefits:

Benefits of capturing design experience

- It helps avoid repeating errors of previous projects;

- it can introduce new team members to a project;

- and it can be used for training and education of newcomers to the field.

Therefore, it has a strong business case, as leaving employees otherwise often take most of the memory and experience from their projects with them, and the enterprise cannot refer to that knowledge anymore to handle similar problems in subsequent projects more efficiently.

A common approach to expressing such experience is in the form of *design guidelines*. However, they usually fall into one of the following two categories:

Guidelines

- *Abstract guidelines*, such as the four design process principles by Gould et al. [1997] or the Eight Golden Rules of Interface Design by Shneiderman [1998, p. 74], are valuable in principle, and they can be applied easily to judge a design a posteriori. It is usually easy to pin down a bad design to the breach of one or several of those rules. However, these guidelines do not suggest constructively how to solve a design problem when the designer is faced with it. They also do not create a vocabulary of applicable solutions, and therefore do not solve the "language" problem.

- *Concrete guidelines*, such as the Macintosh Human Interface Guidelines [Apple Computer, 1992] or the OSF/Motif Style Guide [Open Software Foundation, 1992], are too much tailored to the use of a certain set or *toolkit* of user interface objects. This renders them obsolete relatively quickly, unless the designer takes up the extra work of trying to extract the "timeless" qualities from those specific guidelines.

Even the comprehensive analysis of the field of participatory design [Muller et al., 1997] does not list any methods geared towards capturing general design experience, or design lessons learned during a project.

1.4   A Pattern Framework

To solve the problems outlined above, this book suggests a unified framework to express design experience. It is especially suited to HCI, but also to software engineering, and to the application domain of a project.

The underlying model is formally structured in a hypertext graph notation, to convey a clear understanding of the structure, and to simplify computer support for handling complete instantiations of this framework. However, since the format is intended to support cooperation within the design team, human readability remains paramount and was not sacrificed for formalism.

The framework is based on the idea of languages of design patterns. Put simply, a *design pattern* is a structured textual and graphical description of a proven solution to a recurring design problem. A *pattern language* is a hierarchy of design patterns ordered by their scope. High-level patterns address large-scale design issues and reference lower-level patterns to describe their solution.

Design patterns and pattern languages

The concept originated in urban architecture [Alexander et al., 1977, Alexander, 1979], but has been adapted quite successfully to software engineering, although some of its basic aspects were lost in the process (see chapter 2).

From architecture, to software engineering and HCI, to the application domain

This book extends the notion of pattern languages to two new fields: Firstly, to the discipline of Human–Computer Interaction. Here, design patterns are shown to be a very suitable tool to capture user interface design experience.

Secondly, and an entirely new concept, the pattern language approach is carried over to the application domain of the project. Concepts from the discipline in which the software will be used are also expressed as design patterns ordered into a pattern language.

The pattern framework has been used in a series of design projects dealing with interactive exhibits. Pattern languages from the software engineering, HCI, and application domains of those projects are presented in this book, as well as the design of a sample authoring and browsing tool to work with pattern languages.

1.5   How This Book Is Organized

The rest of this work is organized as follows:

Chapter 2 gives an overview of the history of pattern languages in architecture and software engineering, summarizes the state of the art of pattern languages in HCI, and

State of the art

gives requirements for a pattern-based approach to interaction design.

The pattern
framework

Chapter 3 introduces the central idea of this text, the interdisciplinary pattern language framework to capture and express design experience in HCI, software engineering, and the project's application domain. It gives a formal hypertext model of design patterns and pattern languages, embeds it into an established usability engineering lifecycle model, and discusses how this framework can be used to support design, training, and education in interactive systems design.

Example

Chapter 4 presents an example of this framework, drawn from the author's project experience. It includes a pattern language about HCI design for interactive exhibits drawn from a series of such projects, a pattern language about music as used in the *WorldBeat* exhibit, and several software engineering patterns drawn from those interactive music systems. The HCI pattern language presented here applies to a wide range of scenarios, such as designing public interactive multimedia kiosks and similar systems.

Evaluation and Tool
Support

Chapter 5 evaluates the framework proposed. It compares it with the initial set of requirements, shows results of a peer review of a typical pattern from one of the languages, examines the design and success of resulting pattern-based systems such as the *WorldBeat* exhibit, and evaluates the use of the framework in subsequent projects and in education. It also presents the design of *PET*, a Pattern Editing Tool to write, review, and use pattern languages.

Summary

Chapter 6 summarizes the main contributions of this work, and concludes with directions for further research.

Appendices

After the bibliography, appendix A lists online references made in the text. Appendix B shows a sample run of the *WorldBeat* exhibit that is frequently referred to throughout the text. Finally, a List of Figures and Credits lists the images used in the book and their sources, and the Index contains important terms with pointers to relevant pages in the text.

Chapter 2

Design Pattern Languages

"Every place is given its character by certain patterns of events that keep on happening there. These patterns of events are always interlocked with certain geometric patterns in the space."

—Christopher Alexander, "The Timeless Way of Building"

2.1 Pattern Languages in Architecture

During the renaissance age, architecture, like many other sciences and arts, experienced one of its prime ages. A major key for this revolution was the fact that "master builders" of that time were beginning to systematically collect, document, and structure architectural design knowledge [de Haas, 1999]. A particularly prominent example was master builder Francesco di Giorgio (1439–1501), who led such an effort in Siena. The central ingredient of his documents (see Fig. 2.1) was the *sketch* of a successful design solution, supported by textual explanations, which essentially led to a new literary form, the first "design pattern".

Patterns in renaissance architecture

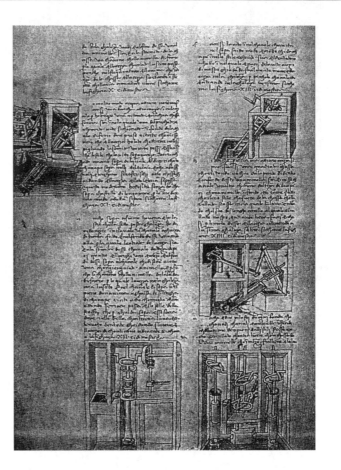

Figure 2.1: A page from *Tratato I* (Francesco di Giorgio, 1480), with constructions for various application domains as well as building and usage information [de Haas, 1999].

In line with this general idea, and out of dissatisfaction with modern urban architecture, a new theory of architecture, building and planning was proposed by architect Christopher Alexander in the 1970s, centred around the idea of *pattern languages*.

Christopher
Alexander

The discussion of Alexander's concept of patterns in architecture below may seem very detailed. Many central concepts and properties of patterns, however, are introduced in this section, and will be used in the subsequent definitions of pattern languages in HCI and other domains.

The pattern idea in architecture

In the first volume of his central work, *The Timeless Way of Building* [Alexander, 1979], architect Christopher Alexander argues that buildings and towns that people enjoy living in have a certain, timeless *Quality Without a Name* that cannot be reduced to a single dimension. Instead, the design of these environments has succeeded in supporting the *patterns of events* that frequently happen there, by implementing a number of according *geometric patterns*, or relationships between their spatial constituents:

Quality Without a Name

> "A building or town is given its character, essentially, by those events that keep on happening there most often."
> [Alexander, 1979, pp. 65–66]

Good spatial patterns within buildings and towns are mostly created not by architects, but rather by the inhabitants themselves. Those environment "users", therefore, have a number of *design patterns* in their heads — often without being able to name them explicitly—which they use to create such suitable environments for themselves.

Inhabitants create better environments

These patterns generally solve a problem of conflicting "forces", or interests. For example, people inside a room are naturally drawn towards the light, and to the window, but they also like to sit down after a while. If a room has only seating in its middle, these forces cannot be resolved. The solution is to build a WINDOW PLACE, some kind of seating, into the window area that allows people to sit very close or inside the window [Alexander et al., 1977, p. 833]. Of course, these forces can also be of a social, economic, natural, or physical nature.

Forces

These patterns have become lost in contemporary society: inhabitants have stopped devising their own environments, and this task has been passed on to dedicated architects and builders. However, these professionals are no longer personally or otherwise closely connected to the future inhabitants of their designs and artefacts. The resulting designs cannot support the users' patterns of habits, tasks, and events in an ideal way.

Patterns are for users

To recreate this shared knowledge of appropriate and good design solutions for buildings, towns, and construction, Alexander describes how these patterns can be made explicit, noted down, tested, and gradually improved. The goal is to re-enable inhabitants to participate in the design of their environments. This is strikingly similar to the idea of participatory design, which aims to actively involve end users in all stages of the software development cycle.

Patterns form a language

Patterns are not isolated: they refer to other, smaller-scale patterns for the solution they describe, and they can only be used in a certain type of context, which is the result of applying larger-scale patterns. This links patterns together to form a hierarchical *pattern language* for the design of a certain building, and further to a language for the design of a whole town.

Design is unfolding, not combining

When this pattern language is shared and used by a whole community, suitable patterns can be applied at all levels of design, from town planning to the rebuilding of a single room in a building. Alexander considers design and building not a process in which preformed parts are combined, but rather an unfolding process in which space is differentiated to create a complex solution.

Piecemeal growth

By applying a sequence of such patterns, entire buildings and towns are gradually created. They are iteratively magnified, fixed, and improved by a process of *piecemeal growth*, again applying patterns to change existing buildings and neighbourhoods, which slowly generates the aforementioned timeless quality in an environment. In fact, Alexander sees his formulated patterns only as a means to remind people of important issues in environmental design; once understood, the patterns have fulfilled their purpose and are, in the long run, no longer needed as a formal framework:

Patterns are only a medium

"Indeed this ageless character has nothing, in the end, to do with languages. The language,

and the processes which stem from it, merely
release the fundamental order which is native
to us. They do not teach us, they only remind
us of what we know already[...]."
[Alexander, 1979,p. 531]

Until this end goal has been reached, however, pattern languages, then, aim to provide laymen with a vocabulary that
helps them to express their ideas and designs, and discuss
them with others. This work essentially carries this idea
over from architecture to user interface design, and to the
application domain, leading to an interdisciplinary design
process where the interface is not designed just by HCI
professionals, but by application domain experts and software designers as well—who can be considered "laymen"
in terms of user interface design.

Architectural pattern examples

The second volume of Alexander's series, *A Pattern Language: Towns, Buildings, Construction* [Alexander et al.,
1977] is an example of his approach. It presents 253 design patterns of "user-friendly" solutions to recurring problems in urban architecture. They range from large-scale
issues (COMMUNITY OF 7000, IDENTIFIABLE NEIGHBOUR-
HOOD), via smaller-scale patterns (PROMENADE, STREET
CAFE) down to patterns for the design of single buildings (CASCADE OF ROOFS, INTIMACY GRADIENT, SITTING
WALL). In [Alexander et al., 1988], the architect uses his
pattern language to define a new planning process for the
University of Oregon as an example.

253 patterns for architecture

The best way to understand what a pattern in the Alexandrian meaning is supposed to be, is to look at some examples from his original collection. The following pages show
two sample patterns from [Alexander et al., 1977], STREET
CAFE and SITTING WALL. Take a moment to read through
these two patterns, and note how they convey their ideas

Examples: STREET CAFE and SITTING WALL

by combining a very structured representation with good readability.

88 STREET CAFE**

... neighborhoods are defined by IDENTIFIABLE NEIGHBORHOOD (14); their natural points of focus are given by ACTIVITY NODES (30) and SMALL PUBLIC SQUARES (61). This pattern, and the ones which follow it, give the neighborhood and its points of focus, their identity.

✣ ✣ ✣

The street cafe provides a unique setting, special to cities: a place where people can sit lazily, legitimately, be on view, and watch the world go by.

The most humane cities are always full of street cafes. Let us try to understand the experience which makes these places so attractive.

We know that people enjoy mixing in public, in parks, squares, along promenades and avenues, in street cafes. The preconditions seem to be: the setting gives you the right to be there, by custom; there are a few things to do that are part of the scene, almost ritual: reading the newspaper, strolling, nursing a beer, playing catch; and people feel safe enough to relax, nod at each other, perhaps even meet. A good cafe terrace meets these conditions. But it has in addition, special qualities of its own: a person may sit there for hours—in public! Strolling, a person must keep up a pace; loitering is only for a few minutes. You can sit still in a park, but there is not the volume of people passing, it is more a private, peaceful experience. And sitting at home on one's porch is again different: it is far more protected; and there is not the mix of people passing by. But on the cafe terrace, you can sit still, relax, and be *very* public. As an experience it has special possibilities; "perhaps the next person . . ."; it is a risky place.

It is this experience that the street cafe supports. And it is one of the attractions of cities, for only in cities do we have the concentration of people required to bring it off. But this experience need not be confined to the special, extraordinary parts of town. In European cities and towns, there is a street cafe in every neighborhood—they are as ordinary as gas stations are in the United

437

436

TOWNS

States. And the existence of such places provides social glue for the community. They become like clubs—people tend to return to their favorite, the faces become familiar. When there is a successful cafe within walking distance of your home, in the neighborhood, so much the better. It helps enormously to increase the identity of a neighborhood. It is one of the few settings where a newcomer to the neighborhood can start learning the ropes and meeting the people who have been there many years.

The ingredients of a successful street cafe seem to be:

1. There is an established local clientele. That is, by name, location, and staff, the cafe is very much anchored in the neighborhood in which it is situated.

2. In addition to the terrace which is open to the street, the cafe contains several other spaces: with games, fire, soft chairs, newspapers. . . . This allows a variety of people to start using it, according to slightly different social styles.

3. The cafe serves simple food and drinks—some alcoholic drinks, but it is not a bar. It is a place where you are as likely to go in the morning, to start the day, as in the evening, for a nightcap.

When these conditions are present, and the cafe takes hold, it offers something unique to the lives of the people who use it: it offers a setting for discussions of great spirit—talks, two-bit lectures, half-public, half-private, learning, exchange of thought.

When we worked for the University of Oregon, we compared the importance of such discussion in cafes and cafe-like places, with the instruction students receive in the classroom. We interviewed 30 students to measure the extent that shops and cafes contributed to their intellectual and emotional growth at the University. We found that "talking with a small group of students in a coffee shop" and "discussion over a glass of beer" scored as high and higher than "examinations" and "laboratory study." Apparently the informal activities of shops and cafes contribute as much to the growth of students, as the more formal educational activities.

We believe this phenomenon is general. The quality that we tried to capture in these interviews, and which is present in a neighborhood cafe, is essential to all neighborhoods—not only student neighborhoods. It is part of their life-blood.

88 STREET CAFE

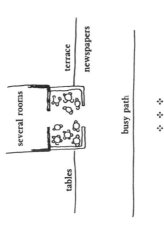

Therefore:

Encourage local cafes to spring up in each neighborhood. Make them intimate places, with several rooms, open to a busy path, where people can sit with coffee or a drink and watch the world go by. Build the front of the cafe so that a set of tables stretch out of the cafe, right into the street.

❖ ❖ ❖

Build a wide, substantial opening between the terrace and the indoors—OPENING TO THE STREET (165); make the terrace double as A PLACE TO WAIT (150) for nearby bus stops and offices; both indoors and on the terrace use a great variety of different kinds of chairs and tables—DIFFERENT CHAIRS (251); and give the terrace some low definition at the street edge if it is in danger of being interrupted by street action—STAIR SEATS (125), SITTING WALL (243), perhaps a CANVAS ROOF (244). For the shape of the building, the terrace, and the surroundings, begin with BUILDING COMPLEX (95). . . .

. . . if all is well, the outdoor areas are largely made up of positive spaces—POSITIVE OUTDOOR SPACES (106); in some fashion you have marked boundaries between gardens and streets, between terraces and gardens, between outdoor rooms and terraces, between play areas and gardens—GREEN STREETS (51), PEDESTRIAN STREET (100), HALF-HIDDEN GARDEN (111), HIERARCHY OF OPEN SPACE (114), PATH SHAPE (121), ACTIVITY POCKETS (124), PRIVATE TERRACE ON THE STREET (140), OUTDOOR ROOM (163), OPENING TO THE STREET (165), GALLERY SURROUND (166), GARDEN GROWING WILD (172). With this pattern, you can help these natural boundaries take on their proper character, by building walls, just low enough to sit on, and high enough to mark the boundaries.

If you have also marked the places where it makes sense to build seats—SEAT SPOTS (241), FRONT DOOR BENCH (242)—you can kill two birds with one stone by using the walls as seats which help enclose the outdoor space wherever its positive character is weakest.

❖ ❖ ❖

In many places walls and fences between outdoor spaces are too high; but no boundary at all does injustice to the subtlety of the divisions between the spaces.

Consider, for example, a garden on a quiet street. At least somewhere along the edge between the two there is a need for a seam, a place which unites the two, but does so without breaking down the fact that they are separate places. If there is a high wall or a hedge, then the people in the garden have no way of being connected to the street; the people in the street have no way of being connected to the garden. But if there is no barrier at all—then the division between the two is hard to maintain. Stray dogs can wander in and out at will; it is even uncomfortable to sit in the garden, because it is essentially like sitting in the street.

243 SITTING WALL**

243   SITTING WALL

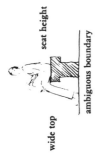

wide top   seat height

ambiguous boundary

❖ ❖ ❖

Place the walls to coincide with natural seat spots, so that extra benches are not necessary—SEAT SPOTS (241); make them of brick or tile, if possible—SOFT TILE AND BRICK (248); if they separate two areas of slightly different height, pierce them with holes to make them balustrades—ORNAMENT (249). Where they are in the sun, and can be large enough, plant flowers in them or against them—RAISED FLOWERS (245). . . . .

CONSTRUCTION

The problem can only be solved by a kind of barrier which functions as a barrier which separates, and as a seam which joins, at the same time.

A low wall or balustrade, just at the right height for sitting, is perfect. It creates a barrier which separates. But because it invites people to sit on it—invites them to sit first with their legs on one side, then with their legs on top, then to swivel round still further to the other side, or to sit astride it—it also functions as a seam, which makes a positive connection between the two places.

Examples: A low wall with the children's sandbox on one side, circulation path on the other; low wall at the front of the garden, connecting the house to the public path; a sitting wall that is a retaining wall, with plants on one side, where people can sit close to the flowers and eat their lunch.

Ruskin describes a sitting wall he experienced:

Last summer I was lodging for a little while in a cottage in the country, and in front of my low window there were, first, some beds of daisies, then a row of gooseberry and currant bushes, and then a low wall about three feet above the ground, covered with stonecress. Outside, a corn-field, with its green ears glistening in the sun, and a field path through it, just past the garden gate. From my window I could see every peasant of the village who passed that way, with basket on arm for market, or spade on shoulder for field. When I was inclined for society, I could lean over my wall, and talk to anybody; when I was inclined for science, I could botanize all along the top of my wall—there were four species of stone-cress alone growing on it; and when I was inclined for exercise, I could jump over my wall, backwards and forwards. That's the sort of fence to have in a Christian country; not a thing which you can't walk inside of without making yourself look like a wild beast, nor look at out of your window in the morning without expecting to see somebody impaled upon it in the night. (John Ruskin, *The Two Paths*, New York: Everyman's Library, 1907, p. 203.)

Therefore:

Surround any natural outdoor area, and make minor boundaries between outdoor areas with low walls, about 16 inches high, and wide enough to sit on, at least 12 inches wide.

The structure of patterns

Uniform pattern
structure

A central property of patterns that becomes visible when studying the above examples is their uniform structure and format. Each of Alexander's patterns consists of the same components, presented in the same sequence and form [Alexander et al., 1977, p. x]:

- the *name* of the pattern,

- a *ranking* of its validity,

- a *picture* as an example of its application,

- the *context* in which it is to be used,

- a short *problem statement*,

- a more detailed *problem description* with empirical background,

- the central *solution* of the pattern,

- a *diagram* illustrating the solution,

- and finally *references* to smaller patterns.

3 larger parts

Name, ranking, picture, and context create the *introductory part* of each pattern. Problem statement, problem description, solution and diagram form its *central part*, and the references are its *closing part*. These major parts of each pattern are divided in the text as well, by lines of three asterisks.

Name

The *name* of a pattern, such as SITTING WALL, is an essential component: it has to convey the idea of the pattern in one or a few words, to make it easy to remember and refer to when thinking about or discussing design solutions.

Ranking

The name is followed by a *ranking* of zero, one, or two asterisks, which indicate the degree of confidence that the authors had in the pattern. No asterisk means that there are certainly ways of solving the problem different from the was described in the pattern: the solution given is more of an example, and the true invariant of the pattern still has to be found.

One asterisk means that the authors believe that some progress has been made towards finding an invariant pattern, but the user is nevertheless encouraged to carefully look for alternative solutions to the problem at hand.

Patterns with two asterisks, finally, are believed to describe a true invariant: the authors are very confident that it is not possible to solve the stated problem without shaping the environment in a way that somehow follows the given solution. The patterns shown above are all from this last group.

Directly after the heading, a *picture* gives an example of the pattern applied. It is usually a photograph of an environment that represents a good example of the idea of the pattern. Our examples include photographs of a typical STREET CAFE, and a typical SITTING WALL.   Picture

The *context* explains which larger-scale patterns this specific pattern helps to implement. This links the pattern to other patterns of a higher level. For example, the STREET CAFE is used to further elaborate the larger-scale pattern of an IDENTIFIABLE NEIGHBOURHOOD.   Context

Three asterisks now mark the beginning of the central part of each pattern.   ***

Next, a short *problem statement* summarizes the general situation that the pattern addresses. The problem statement of the SITTING WALL pattern, for example, shows that this pattern addresses the conflict between the necessity to divide open spaces, and the disconnecting nature of high walls.   Problem statement

A more extensive *problem description* follows that gives empirical background information on the pattern. It often states the problem using the concept of competing "forces" described earlier. In the SITTING WALL example, these forces are to build higher walls, and to build lower or no walls. The goal of the pattern is to resolve, or balance, these forces optimally in the given context: Problem description

> "As an element in the world, each pattern is a relationship between a certain context, a certain system of forces which occurs repeatedly in that context, and a certain spatial configuration which allows these forces to resolve themselves.
>
> As an element of language, a pattern is an instruction, which shows how this spatial configuration can be used, over and over again, to resolve the given system of forces, wherever the context makes it relevant."
>
> [Alexander, 1979, p. 247]

The problem description also discusses existing solutions.

Solution

The next and central component of each pattern is a statement that distils, from those examples, a general *solution* to the problem at hand. It is a clear, but generic, set of instructions that can be applied in varying situations.

Diagram

The solution is visualized, and made easier to grasp and remember, with a simple *diagram* of its central idea. It sketches the solution and its major constituents graphically. Since every pattern is supposed to describe a spatial configuration to solve a certain problem, sketching a pattern must always be possible:

> "If you can't draw a diagram of it, it isn't a pattern."
>
> [Alexander, 1979, p. 267]

***

References

Three more asterisks mark the end of the central part of the pattern, and are followed by its last component, the *references*, which point the reader to smaller patterns. These are other patterns that the author recommends in order to implement and further "unfold" the solution of the current pattern. The STREET CAFE pattern, for example, suggests to use a SITTING WALL to separate the terrace from the street.

Implicit Structuring Through Typography

Alexander's patterns do not contain explicit text tags for
each part of each pattern: there is no label saying "Context:", or "Solution:". Though this may seem at first as if
this structuring is missing, looking at the patterns more
closely reveals that this structural information is commu-
nicated *implicitly*, using very rigid rules of typography. The
most important rules are:

No explicit labels

- Each pattern contains the same parts, in the same order: it starts with a name, followed by ranking, opening picture, context, etc., up to the last part of each
  pattern, its references.

Typographical rules

- Each pattern part is always typeset or rendered in the
  same way: the name in small capitals, the problem
  and solution in bold face as separate paragraphs, the
  diagram as a hand-drawn sketch, etc.

- Special words or signs are used to further distinguish
  each pattern part: the context begins with an initial
  ellipsis (...), which also ends the references, the solution is introduced with the word "Therefore:" on a
  separate line, and three asterisks open and close the
  pattern "body" between context and references.

This implicit structuring makes it unnecessary to clutter the
text with distracting, repetitive, and typographically unaesthetic labels. At the same time, it is still possible to determine immediately, for example, that a paragraph in bold
face following the word "Therefore" *must* be the solution
part of a pattern.

Closer examination shows that, in Alexander's pattern language, not every reference to a smaller-scale pattern is reflected in a corresponding backward link in the context section of that pattern. The graph of links that point downwards in the hierarchy is different from the graph of those
that point upwards. However, it must be stressed that

Consistency of
references

Alexandrian patterns are, above all, a didactic medium for human readers, even (and especially) for non-architects. To Alexander, this quality has priority over a mathematically "correct" representation. It also must not be lost in a more formal representation.

Interestingly, Alexander's ideas were not always received well by his colleagues. One reason for this is that Alexander's concepts empowered the inhabitants, supplying them with more ways to influence the building process, and taking much of that power out of the hands of the professional. Obviously, this idea was not very popular among architects.

2.2   Pattern Languages in Software Engineering

The Smalltalk experiment

In 1987, software engineering picked up the idea of using pattern languages from architecture to express design experience. At the OOPSLA conference on object-orientation, Beck and Cunningham [1987] reported on an experiment where application domain experts without prior Smalltalk experience quite successfully designed their own Smalltalk user interfaces. These users had been introduced to basic Smalltalk UI concepts using a pattern language of just five basic patterns. One of these patterns, COLLECT LOW-LEVEL PROTOCOL, is given below in abbreviated form:

> "Once you have initially decomposed a system into objects [Objects from the User's World] and refined the objects [Engines and Holders] you need to begin collecting useful functionality that doesn't particularly fit into any single object. Often many objects need to communicate with low-level (bit- or byte-oriented) parts of the system. For example, external files can have complex or highly encoded formats that

require substantial byte or even bit manipulation to interpret. Collect all necessary protocol for decoding file formats or any other particular low-level task into an object specifically
designed for the purpose. Do so even if you
might otherwise spread it around several other
objects. Once you have done this you are ready
to begin testing and refining your objects [Ele-
gance through Debugging]."

> [Beck and Cunningham, 1987]

Due to its more technical terms, this pattern is not quite as
easy to understand as a typical pattern from Alexander's
collection. Nevertheless, it is interesting to note that this
first software pattern experiment actually dealt with user
interface design, and user participation. It was therefore
still relatively close to the original goals of the pattern approach.

The OOPSLA workshop started a vivid exchange about
software design patterns. An influential collection of patterns for object-oriented software design was published by
the "Gang of Four" [Gamma et al., 1995]. Although it is
generally regarded as the archetype of a software patterns
book, it does not entirely fulfil the demands of a pattern
language as intended by Alexander: the collection, and the
linking between the individual patterns, is not complete
enough to be a language. Furthermore, many patterns do
not represent the knowledge and concepts of good object-
oriented design as gained by expertise, but rather work-
arounds to implement object-oriented concepts despite the
shortcomings of today's programming languages, such as
C++. But above all, they are not written with the idea of empowering users to participate in the design process in mind.
Typical patterns from the collection dedicate over fifty per-
cent of their text to implementation details and sample code
listings. A professional programmer can learn a lot from
these patterns to improve his program design and implementation skills, but they are not intended for a more general audience.

The Gang Of Four book: A pattern language?

PLoP conferences:
few work on HCI

However, many other researchers have developed ideas about how to adopt the pattern principle for software engineering, and the annual Pattern Languages of Programming (PLoP) conferences [Coplien and Schmidt, 1995, Vlissides et al., 1996, Martin et al., 1998, Harrison et al., 1999] have succeeded in establishing an entirely new and useful forum to exchange proven, generalized solutions to recurring software design problems among professionals.

The field of human–computer interaction, however, is hardly touched upon in this series, with only a few notable exceptions:

Riehle and Züllighoven [1995] describe a pattern language for their "tools and materials" design metaphor. Their abstract patterns, or *design metaphors*, describe a quite human-centred, task-oriented concept of HCI design, although their concrete *design patterns* are firmly rooted in the more technical approach of Gamma et al. [1995].

Rossi et al. [1996] present two design patterns to model navigation in hypermedia systems. NAVIGATION STRATEGY decouples link activation from computing the link target. NAVIGATION OBSERVER simplifies navigation history management by separating the objects recording navigation from the actual contents. The work has been continued in [Rossi et al., 1997]. The problems that those patterns address, however, are again very much in the software engineering domain.

The third volume of this series is the first one to explicitly contain a part on user interface patterns. However, the introduction to this part voices an interesting concern that HCI issues might have been overlooked by the community before:

> "This part contains only one chapter, which is remarkable and puzzling. In a field that has brought us patterns such as Observer, Model-View-Controller, Taskmaster, and so forth, we would have expected this type of pattern to flourish. Aren't there any more user interface

> patterns to be found? Have we really exhausted
> this field? Perhaps this is an indication that this
> field needs more work, and many patterns are
> still waiting to be discovered." [Martin et al.,
> 1998, p. 345]

The language presented in that volume [Bradac and
Fletcher, 1998] helps with constructing forms-based user interfaces. As with the other HCI-oriented PLoP pattern languages, it instructs a developer how to implement a certain
type of interface in an elegant and efficient way. It does
not give instructions to a user interface designer (or even
somebody from another domain) regarding which types or
combinations of user interface components should be used
for which tasks. Similar work has been carried out by Nanard et al. [1998], who use design patterns and "constructive templates" to capture structures and components for
reuse in hypermedia design and development.

In all, the overall format of a pattern has not changed very
much from Alexander et al. [1977] to, for example, Gamma
et al. [1995]. Name, context, problem, solution, examples,
diagrams, and cross-references are still the essential constituents of each pattern. The goals have, however, changed
in an important way, without many noticing:

Software design patterns are considered a useful language
for communication *among software designers*, and a practical
vehicle for introducing less experienced designers into the
field. The idea of end users designing their own (software)
architectures has not been taken over. On the one hand,
this makes sense, because people do not live as intensely
"in" their software applications as they live in their environments. On the other hand, though, a good chance to
push the concepts of participatory design and work ethics
forward by introducing patterns has not been taken advantage of. Alexander summarizes this in his keynote speech
at OOPSLA'96:

*Software patterns
are not for users*

> "Now, my understanding of what you are
> doing with patterns... It is a kind of a neat for-

mat, and that is fine. The pattern language that
we began did have other features, and I don't
know whether those have translated into your
discipline. I mean, there was at root behind the
whole thing a continuous mode of preoccupa-
tion with under what circumstances is the environment good. In our field that means something."

[Alexander, 1996]

2.3   Pattern Languages in HCI

This section summarizes most previous research that has
been carried out in the field of pattern languages for
human–computer interaction. It serves as an overview of
the state of the art in this area.

Early pattern references in HCI

HCI has looked at
Alexander before
software engineering

In the academic and professional field of HCI, the idea of
design patterns has received much less attention than in
software engineering. Nevertheless, Alexander's pattern
approach has been referenced by HCI research earlier than
one would expect—earlier, actually, than its first widely
known appearance in software engineering at the OOPSLA
1987 conference [Beck and Cunningham, 1987].

Norman about
patterns

Probably the earliest HCI-oriented reference to Alexander's
pattern idea can be found in Norman and Draper's seminal
book on user-centred system design [Norman and Draper,
1986]. Shortly afterwards, in his text on the design of everyday products [Norman, 1988], which is also a standard
work among user interface researchers and practitioners,
Norman explains that he was influenced particularly by
Alexander's work:

"All of Alexander's works describe [a] process of evolution, and his books on architectural

design are influential. [...] I find the works
fascinating to skim, frustrating to read, and difficult to put into practice, but his descriptions
of the structure of homes and villages are very
good."

                                   [Norman, 1988, p. 229]

Another classic HCI text, Apple Computer's *Macintosh Hu-*   Macintosh Human
man Interface Guidelines, quotes Alexander's work as semi-   Interface Guidelines
nal in the field of environmental design in its list of recom-
mended reading for user interface designers [Apple Computer, 1992, p. 338].

In a more educational context, Barfield et al. [1994] describe   Utrecht's
how they used the pattern approach in their interaction   pattern-based
design curriculum at the Utrecht School of Arts. The au-   curriculum
thors argue that computer users work as active agents inside evolving information ecologies, and that many of the
systems they use work not in isolation, but as parts of larger
networks. This establishes important links from HCI design to architecture and urban design. In both architecture
and HCI, the central issues in the relation between user and
environment, whether physical or virtual, are:

- how users experience an environment,

- how an environment influences individual behaviour,

- how single environments integrate into the larger
  context, and

- how these smaller and larger environments develop
  and change over time.

Barfield et al. state that, as for architecture (see p. 11), the
important thing in a user interface is not its form, but what
happens inside it. Patterns refer to relationships between
physical elements and the events that happen there. Interface designers, like urban architects, strive to create environments that establish certain behavioural patterns with

a positive effect onto those people "inside" these environments. The "Quality Without a Name" that Alexander demands of good, "timeless" architecture is comparable to user interface qualities such as "transparent" and "natural".

In their curriculum, Barfield et al. establish patterns, like Alexander, as three-part rules with context, forces, and configuration. Most user interface "guidelines" function like patterns, and the pattern form can be used to phrase guidelines in a *consistent format* that leaves room for subtleties; for example, "When users have to wait for a certain period of time (context), this can be frustrating because we don't know what's going on (forces), so be sure to provide feedback on the system's progress (abstract configuration)." [Barfield et al., 1994, p. 72].

HCI patterns need to model time as well as space.

They also point out, however, that interaction design is quite different from architecture in one important way: time is an essential component. Interaction is much more dynamic, and context and system of forces often change during the course of interaction.

Nevertheless, a trio of interaction design courses in their curriculum is based successfully on the pattern concept. Students do exercises such as finding interaction designs with and without the "quality without a name", defining patterns based on their observations, and transforming interface guidelines into patterns.

HCI patterns: more natural than software patterns

In all, these references, especially the work by Barfield et al. [1994], show that the importance of the "quality without a name", and the influence of design decisions on the users' experience of their environment, is even more evident in interaction design than in software engineering, which justifies the following *statement:*

> *The notion of design patterns, as it was intended in architecture, carries over more naturally to user interface design than it does to software design.*

Recent research efforts

Since 1997, the subject of pattern languages in HCI has begun to be addressed more intensively. From a workshop at CHI'97, the largest annual HCI conference, Bayle et al. [1998] report that the ideas about adopting the pattern concept for HCI are still very varied. Even the notion of a "pattern" is being used in two senses: as *design pattern* in the sense of the present text, but also as *activity pattern* that simply describes an existing situation as it is, without claiming that it has any special quality or value to be reused and preserved. The latter definition makes sense especially when describing *organizational patterns* that capture structures and workflows in an organization. Accordingly, it identifies many different ways of using patterns in HCI [Bayle et al., 1998]:

CHI'97 workshop: Design or activity patterns?

Capture and Description: describe key characteristics of a situation or event in a context-sensitive way;

Generalization: generalize across varying situations, yet retain a certain concreteness;

Prescription: give prescriptive guidelines for common problems in HCI (or organizational) design;

Rhetoric: create the vocabulary for a *lingua franca*, a common language, between designers and users; or

Prediction: judge potential consequences of design changes to an existing system or environment, by following ramifications through the pattern network.

The patterns described by the workshop follow the idea of activity patterns and address solutions observed at the conference location. They include, for example:

CHI '97 workshop example patterns

ADMINISTRATIVE NEXUS IN THE EDDY. This pattern describes the problem of locating the conference office. Forces include the necessity to be near the loci of most frequent or severe problems, but also to be not so prominent as to attract casual, non-crucial requests. The solution observed is to place it near the conference area, but far enough away that it is not noticed by people unless they are looking for it. An example of this was the CHI '97 conference office.

CLARIFICATION GRAFFITI. This pattern describes the problem that signs are often meaningless to users because of the different perspective and context of sign designer and user. Forces include the necessity to create aesthetically pleasing signs in advance, but also to experience the actual context when the sign is in use in order to make it meaningful to readers. The solution is that users often add their own notes to existing signs in order to make them more understandable for fellow users. An example at the conference was a printed sign "Message Board on Ballroom Level", which someone had clarified with a handwritten note "(go up one floor)."

The second example especially shows the workshop's tendency toward activity patterns: the pattern describes a solution that is not one to strive for in future designs; rather, it tells the designer what real-world behaviour to expect and take into account when creating similar signs. The pattern could be applied in two ways: either by trying to make sure that signs are meaningful in their final context, thereby eliminating the use of clarification graffiti; or by accepting that it will always be impossible to phrase signs optimally until they are put into use, and consciously permitting for on-site clarification graffiti, for example by leaving space on signs for additional directions, etc.

Erickson: Interaction patterns to describe workplaces

One of the workshop organizers has subsequently refined these ideas [Erickson, 1998]. Erickson aims to use patterns as a way to *describe workplaces*, and provide a "what-if" mechanism to reflect about design options. This should make it easier for stakeholders (the various groups engaged in interdisciplinary design, including potential users) to identify important recurring design problems and solutions. Patterns can enable stakeholders to talk about and participate in design, and allow for the creation of shared, social artefacts that these stakeholders can use. Ultimately, interaction pattern languages can be a *lingua franca*, legitimizing and empowering "users", and also increasing accessibility of research results.

Thus, Erickson's notion of *Interaction Design Patterns* primarily refers to human–human, not human–computer interaction. In [Erickson, 1998], he is quite clear about the fact that his major interest in patterns is *not* to capture known design solutions in a general way, to support training and discussion within a design organization, or to achieve the "Quality Without a Name". Nevertheless, he recognizes the idea that other research efforts are looking at the pattern idea for those reasons and consequentially applying them to user interface design and implementation. As a consequence, he has established the first *Interaction Patterns Home Page* [H:Erickson98], a very useful collection of publications and pattern collections in human–human and human–computer interaction.

A number of concrete pattern collections for interaction design have been suggested. Currently, the language by Tidwell [1998] is the most comprehensive effort in this field. It addresses the general problem of designing an interactive software artefact, deliberately leaving aside implementation issues for specific user interface technologies, although these are mentioned in the examples section of each pattern.

The language goes beyond pattern efforts in the software community such as the collection by Gamma et al. [1995], and is closer to the Alexandrian ideas of a pattern language, in that it represents timeless principles of good interaction design in a hierarchically structured, interlinked set of patterns that are intended to guide the designer at various levels of abstraction throughout the design process.

According to Tidwell, the success of pattern approaches in architecture and software design calls for an application of

Interaction Patterns
Home Page

Tidwell's HCI pattern
language

the idea to user interface design. Tidwell argues that patterns are a good form to express design guidelines. Typical GUI (Graphical User Interface) style guides are useful to ensure a common look and feel across multiple applications built with a certain user interface toolkit, but they are too much tied to this toolkit, which makes them transient: as soon as the underlying toolkit changes (for example, from Windows 3.1 to Windows 95), their rules become hard to apply, and seem out of date. Moreover, such style guides limit interface design alternatives to those that are supported by the present toolkit, and they do not help the designer to balance multiple high-level design principles in a particular situation. User tests, on the other hand, are useful and necessary throughout the design cycle, but patterns can support the creative process of devising a design in the first place, or of improving a solution after problems were found.

Tidwell sees several benefits that patterns may bring to the individual user interface designer, and to the user interface design community as a whole:

- Patterns can capture the collective wisdom of experienced designers in HCI and related design fields.

- They can supply a common language to the community.

- They allow the designer to think "outside" the toolkit at hand.

- Whereas today, many excellent user interface prototypes never gain wide acceptance, patterns could help to extract the timeless characteristics of these widgets and solutions, and pass them on to the community.

- They may serve as a starting point when implementing new interface toolkits.

- Some patterns may even be encoded in software.

The language in [Tidwell, 1998] consists of more than fifty patterns, plus several more that have not been written in detail yet. The patterns are grouped into different problem subdomains with a varying level of detail, and they mostly address either a question of how to present *content*, or an issue of how to make *actions* available.

Alternatives for the basic shape of the content are described by patterns such as the linear and mostly verbal NARRATIVE form, the HIGH-DENSITY INFORMATION DISPLAY of maps, tables, and charts, and the STATUS DISPLAY found in many electrical appliances.

Overview of Tidwell's patterns

The next set of patterns deals with the basic shape of actions, and includes patterns such as the fill-in FORM, the CONTROL PANEL, for example of a TV remote control, the WYSIWYG EDITOR as found in word processors, the COMPOSED COMMAND used in command-line interfaces such as the UNIX shell, and the online SOCIAL SPACE of newsgroups and chat rooms.

These patterns define the overall appearance and behaviour of the artefact. Subsequently, possible ways to unfold content and actions before the user are discussed in patterns such as highly interactive, self-paced NAVIGABLE SPACES, the tree-like HIERARCHICAL SET display, or the technique that the POINTER SHOWS AFFORDANCE.

A separate set of patterns describes how the system relates to the user's attention (SOVEREIGN POSTURE, HELPER POSTURE, BACKGROUND POSTURE), while others deal with questions of the layout of working areas (CENTRAL, TILED, STACK, or PILE OF WORKING SURFACES) or navigation (GO BACK ONE STEP, GO BACK TO A SAFE PLACE).

The patterns reach down to low-level details such as specific forms of data entry (SLIDING SCALE) and display (PROGRESS INDICATOR), and also deal with questions of customizing and other forms of user support (USER'S ANNOTATIONS, GOOD DEFAULTS).

The following is an example from Tidwell's pattern language.

Tidwell: Pattern
example

GO BACK TO A SAFE PLACE

Examples:

- The "Home" button on a Web browser
- Turning back to the beginning of a chapter in a physical book or magazine
- The "Revert" feature on some computer applications

Context: The artefact allows a user to move through spaces (as in NAVIGABLE SPACES), or steps (as in STEP-BY-STEP INSTRUCTIONS), or a linear NARRATIVE, or discrete states; the artefact also has one or more checkpoints in that set of spaces.

Problem: How can the artefact make navigation easy, convenient, and psychologically safe for the user?

Forces:

- A user that explores a complex artefact, or tries many state-changing operations, may literally get lost.
- A user may forget where they were, if they stop using the artefact while they're in the middle of something and don't get back to it for a while.
- If the user gets into a space or a state that they don't want to be in, they will want to get out of it in a safe and predictable way.
- The user is more likely to explore an artefact if they are assured that they can easily get out of an undesired state or space; that assurance engenders a feeling of security.
- Backtracking out of a long navigation path can be very tedious.

Solution: Provide a way to go back to a checkpoint of the user's choice. That checkpoint may be a home page, a saved file or state, the logical beginning of a section of narrative or a set of steps. Ideally, it could be whatever state or space a user chooses to declare as a checkpoint.

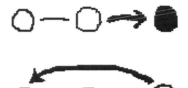

Resulting Context: GO BACK ONE STEP is a natural adjunct to this pattern, and is often found along with it. For non-Narrative use, INTERACTION HISTORY is useful too, almost to the point of making GO BACK TO A SAFE PLACE unnecessary: it may actually help a "lost" user figure out where they are, for instance, or remind an interrupted user of where they are and what they've done.

Tidwell's pattern collection is currently the most promising effort to create an HCI pattern language. While it has a few weaknesses (several of its patterns have not been detailed yet, the pattern format is not always kept consistent, and the collection has not been updated in recent months), it has already served as a frequently quoted example of what an HCI pattern language could look like.

The first workshop in which the pattern communities from software engineering and HCI got into direct contact took place at ChiliPLoP'99, one of the three annual conferences in the PLoP conference series.

CHI meets PLoP: The ChiliPLoP workshop

As a first result, the workshop turned out an initial definition of what interaction patterns are. This definition was arrived at after much discussion, but it also found broad approval by the other pattern people at the conference:

Initial definition:
Interaction Pattern
Language

> "An Interaction Pattern Language generates space/time interaction designs that create a system image close to the user's mental model of the task at hand, to make the human–computer interface as transparent as possible."
>
> [Borchers, 2000a]

The definition was intentionally not expressed to describe what a single interaction pattern is, as the linking between patterns is generally considered at least as important as the individual patterns themselves (see, for example, [Borchers, 2000a] for James Coplien's views on this).

Another important detail of the definition is that it talks about *space/time interaction designs*. This is to stress the temporal dimension of HCI design, as previously described (see p. 28): Alexander's patterns almost exclusively deal with spatial configurations. Human–Computer Interaction, on the other hand, has to take into account that the user interface of an interactive computer system is a dynamic environment that will usually change its appearance and behaviour substantially over the course of an interaction.

The term "transparency" is an approximation of Alexander's "Quality Without a Name" for human–computer interfaces (see p. 28). The definition also aims at putting the user's task into the focus of attention, following the principles of user-centred design.

Initial taxonomy of interaction design patterns:

The second important result of the workshop is an initial taxonomy of interaction design patterns. It distinguishes three main dimensions along which interaction patterns can be classified meaningfully (see Fig. 2.4).

Level of abstraction

The most important dimension is *level of abstraction:* Interaction design patterns can address very large-scale issues that comprise a user's complete *task*, they can address smaller-scale, slightly more concrete topics that describe the *style* of a certain part of the interaction (such as a

BROWSER style), or they can deal with low-level questions of user interface design that look at individual user interface objects (whether virtual or physical).

The inclusion of a fourth layer, "technology", to distinguish the actual input and output hardware considerations, was rejected as the distinction from software objects did not seem useful enough.

The second fundamental dimension is *function:* patterns can be classified into those that address mainly questions of (visual, auditory, etc.) *perception* (interface output), and those that deal with interface input, or, more specifically, *manipulation* of some kind of application data, or *navigation* through the system.

Function

The distinction between navigation and manipulation may seem too software-centred, but this reflects the engineering-oriented nature of the workshop.

The third dimension is *physical dimension:* some patterns will address questions of *spatial* layout, while others deal with issues of *sequence* (discrete series of events, e.g. a sequence of dialogues), or with continuous *time* (such as a design pattern about using animation techniques in the user interface).

Physical dimension

The taxonomy was evaluated by trying to classify patterns from the workshop according to it.

Using the taxonomy

For example, the pattern INCREMENTAL REVEALING from the workshop captures the idea that a user interface for non-expert users should initially appear relatively simple and easy to grasp, and that the system should only reveal additional "depth" (contents or features) when the user becomes active and looks for it. The pattern is described in more detail in [Borchers, 1999].

This pattern lies at a *high level of abstraction:* it addresses how the complete *task* of the user is dealt with. Its *function* lies mainly in *perception*, as it suggests how much information to display or otherwise output to the user. Its *physical dimension* is *sequence*, as it deals with the distribution of this

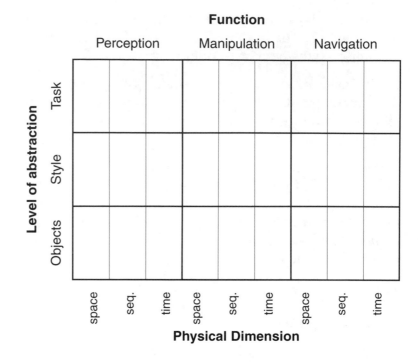

Figure 2.4: A taxonomy of human–computer interaction design patterns. [Borchers, 2000a]

information over a sequence of user events, e.g. subsequent screens of an information system.

Writers' Workshop

The workshop also applied the concept of a *Writers' Workshop* to the interaction patterns submitted, and the entire workshop was considered very successful by participants and outsiders. Nevertheless, it also made clear that the software engineering patterns community requires more input from other disciplines such as HCI.

The results from this Workshop on Interaction Patterns are described in more detail in [Borchers, 2000a][1].

INTERACT'99 workshop

At the INTERACT'99 conference on Human–Computer In-

---

[1]I was the only HCI researcher at that workshop of software engineering people. A good example of the different approaches was that a software system was considered a *problem* that the UI needs to "solve"— whereas HCI usually considers systems to be *solutions* to problems that *users* have. . .

teraction, the next major workshop on the subject was co-organized by the author. It built on the previous findings, and delivered several new results:

The workshop agreed on a "user-centred" definition that describes HCI Pattern Languages by defining what they can be used for.

A user-centred definition

> "The goals of an HCI Pattern Language are
> to share successful HCI design solutions among
> HCI professionals, and to provide a common
> language for HCI design to anyone involved in
> the design, development, evaluation, or use of
> interactive systems."
>
> [Borchers et al., 2001]

Several *organizing principles* for HCI design patterns were conceived and elaborated in more detail. An important point is that the ultimate goal of any organizing principle is to support an iterative design process, with the connections in the patterns hierarchy always leading the designer to the next logical step to consider.

Organizing principles:

The first principle classifies patterns according to *scale*, similarly to Alexander's sorting hierarchy. It has to take into account, though, that the dynamics of user interfaces require incorporating time as well as space into such a classification. The resulting categories were:

Scale principle

- Society (beyond systems)

- Multiple Users

- Social Position

- System

- Application

- UI structure (Dialogue)

- Components (containers, windows, layout)

- Primitives (buttons and other simple widgets)

- Physical properties

An interesting observation is that the real world of technology changes fastest in the middle area of this scale, between system and components. Since patterns are by definition supposed to capture some timeless quality, it may be particularly difficult to write genuine patterns for this area. At the same time, many existing guidelines — and many of the submitted patterns—address exactly this middle level, which may render them obsolete rather quickly.

Process principle

Another possible organizing principle that the workshop developed is to follow the HCI design process, leading from analysis- to structure-oriented patterns:

- The highest level is *culture and society*, followed by *environment* and *role* of the user

- The next levels are *use* and *navigation* (incorporating affordances and, for example, issues of safety versus exploration)

- After those analysis-oriented levels, structural levels follow

- As an example, *tasks* can be further classified into retrieval, monitoring, proactive and reactive controlling, construction (writing a document), transactions, modifications (changing contents or structure), calculation, workflow, and communication.

Using the scale principle

The patterns submitted to that workshop can be sorted according to the above organizing principle of scale:

- An example of patterns at the *Multiple Users* level is Lyn Pemberton's LET PEOPLE OVERHEAR, which addresses issues of cooperative work.

- Patterns at the *System* level include Ger Koelman's EXPLORABLE INTERFACE and Jan Borchers' INCREMENTAL REVEALING, which both deal with the overall impression that a system conveys.

- Patterns that deal with how to design individual applications include Lyn Pemberton's JUST THE USUAL about application vocabulary and Peter Windsor's SITUATION DISPLAY and WORK QUEUE patterns for overall appearance for a certain type of applications.

- Most of our patterns addressed the Dialogue level, such as David England's AVATAR JOINING for temporal UI aspects of virtual worlds, Diane Love's selection patterns CHOICE OF SUBLIST FROM A LARGE LIST and CONFIGURING ORDERED SLOTS IN HARDWARE, and Fernando Lyardet et al.'s INFORMATION ON DEMAND, BEHAVIOUR ANTICIPATION, INFORMATION-INTERACTION DECOUPLING, and BEHAVIOURAL GROUPING patterns for navigation. Richard Griffiths' GIVE A WARNING also falls into this category.

- Patterns describing solutions at the *Components* level include Barbara Mirel's INFORMATION FLOW FOR PRECISION for data visualisation and Janet Louise Wesson's *List Selection* pattern.

- The level of *Primitives* is covered by patterns such as Martin Hitz's SELECTION ITERATOR, which also contains implementation recommendations.

- The *Physical Properties* level contains patterns such as John Thomas' SUPPORT THE HANDS WITH SPECIALIZED TOOLS.

- Some patterns do not address design issues of interactive systems, but rather aspects of the software development process such systems require, and therefore do not fall easily into the above categorization. Examples include Michael Mahemoff's ONLINE REPOSITORY for developing internationalized software.

Interact workshop
pattern example

As an example, the workshop agreed on a definition of a "typical" HCI design pattern, DESCRIPTION AT YOUR FINGERTIPS. It captures the idea of adding temporary information to objects in the user interface to deliver short explanations without permanently cluttering the interface space.

Pattern title

DESCRIPTION AT YOUR FINGERTIPS

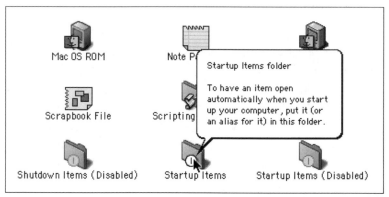

Sensitizing example

Problem statement

You are putting interactive objects on a dynamic medium such as a screen and you want to provide various levels of context sensitive help supporting uninterruptable tasks.

Extensive explanations tend to clutter the interface but users may need such help. They do not want to leave the context of their current task, and experts may not want to see the help at all.

Existing examples

In the Mac OS®, a small balloon of textual help appears when the user turns on this feature and moves the mouse over an object. In Windows Tool Tips, the same happens if the mouse hovers over an object. In Netscape, the URL of a link is displayed in a fixed position at the bottom of the screen if the cursor is moved over it. In a voice mailbox, options are explained if the user waits for a while.

Formation of a
general solution

Therefore: Provide a short description of the object either close to it or in a fixed position. Let users turn it on and off or only provide it on some explicit user action (e.g. hovering).

Alternative representation:

```
On <start trigger>
    give <description>
    at <location>
On <end trigger>
    extinguish <description>
```

Schematic

You can use three-state buttons to implement descriptions like this. Longer explanations can go into on-line help, possibly delivered via an intelligent agent, or in the manual.

Reference to constituent/related patterns

The overall structure follows the Alexandrian format quite closely. It is amended by an alternative, pseudo-code representation of the concept that is more suitable to represent the pattern dynamics over time.

A similar pattern has been described by Tidwell [1998] under the name SHORT DESCRIPTION.

2.4   Pattern Languages in Other Disciplines

One of the claims of this text is that the pattern approach can also be used to model design-like knowledge from the application domain of a software project. To show that it makes sense to look at domains other than architecture, software engineering, and HCI, several examples of pattern approaches for diverse domains are described below.

Patterns and
cognition

The large appeal of the pattern concept may partly be due to the fact that, according to cognitive theory, patterns might be a particularly effective way to organize complex information in general [Barsalou, 1992].

This idea of creating a vocabulary implements the well-known results from psychological research about *verbal recoding*: "When there is a story or an argument or an idea that we want to remember [...], we make a verbal description of the event and then remember our verbalization" [Miller, 1956]. The idea can be recalled when its short name is remembered.

Casaday: Patterns
ubiquitous

Casaday [1997] suggests applying the idea of pattern-based design to the creation of usable interactive systems. He argues that patterns in a broader sense can be found in architecture, organizational behaviour (archetypes), history of science (paradigms), military theory, studies of mythology (archetypes), and even basic text writing (templates). In fact, the software engineering PLoP community even has created a pattern language for the process of writing patterns [Meszaros and Doble, 1998].

Denning: Pattern
mapping

Several others have noticed the potential of pattern languages for interdisciplinary design. Denning and Dargan [1996], for example, in their theory of action-centred design, suggest a technique called *Pattern Mapping* as a basis for cross-disciplinary software design. Referring to Alexander's work, they claim that patterns could constitute a design language for communication between software engineers and users, just as Alexander's pattern language does between builder and inhabitant.

PSA

Granlund and Lafrenière [1999b] use patterns in their pattern-supported approach (PSA) to describe business domains, processes, and tasks, in order to aid early system definition and conceptual design. The authors also note the interdisciplinary value of patterns as a communications medium, and the ability of patterns to capture knowledge from previous projects. The business domain and process patterns are intentionally not patterns in the Alexandrian sense; they do not include a section describing a solution to a problem that they discuss. Consequently, the pattern format used is not uniform. In contrast to Alexander, the patterns are relatively short and not as elaborate.

Their approach served as common ground for a workshop on user interface patterns at the 1999 Usability Professionals' Association (UPA) Conference. The major results of this workshop [Granlund and Lafrenière, 1999a] are summarized below:

UPA'99 workshop

- A distinction between Alexandrian *design patterns,* and *information patterns* was introduced. The latter describe information about user, context, and task, and lack the problem and solution parts.

- The need for *conceptual design patterns,* "blueprint patterns" for the overall conceptual design, was expressed to avoid concentrating on individual parts of a system design.

- The problem of finding the right balance between too generic and too domain-specific patterns was also addressed: for example, patterns describing tasks could be divided into a generic part with "framing forces", pointing to general conceptual design patterns, and a domain-specific part including forces, consequences, and examples that only apply to a concrete domain.

- Finally, a major point stressed by the workshop is that the process of creating and using patterns must not become too mechanistic and complex. Otherwise, the inherent ease-of-use of good patterns would be lost.

Most of the events mentioned above have been collected on the HCI Patterns Home Page [H:Borchers99].

HCI Patterns Home Page

2.5   A Comparison of Central Pattern Collections

While numerous other projects applying the pattern concept to new domains exist, this chapter comprehensively covered the important fields for the present work, especially the area of human–computer interaction.

Alexander, Gamma, and Tidwell

To summarize, here is a table comparing the most notable pattern collections in the various fields discussed above.

Pattern collection	Domain	Components	Format	Uniformity
Alexander et al. [1977]	architecture	name, ranking, picture, context, problem statement, problem description with forces and examples, solution, diagram, references	structured text, photos and diagrams	++
Gamma et al. [1995]	software development	name, classification, intent, aliases, motivation, applicability, structure, participants, collaborations, consequences, implementation, sample code, known uses, related patterns	structured text, diagrams and source code	++
Tidwell [1998]	user interface design	name, examples, context, problem, forces, solution, diagram (sometimes), resulting context, notes	structured text and bullet lists, some diagrams	+

Figure 2.5: Comparing major pattern languages from different domains.

Structural similarity across domains

Comparing the central pattern components and their format across different domains shows that there is indeed a high level of agreement on how a pattern language should be structured. This result will be used in the following chapter to define a domain-independent formal model of pattern languages, leading to the central idea of this work, an interdisciplinary pattern framework for the design of interactive systems.

The comparison also reveals that the selected language for HCI patterns is less uniform in its structure than the examples from the other domain. This is true for most existing HCI pattern efforts, and indicates that the concept of patterns is not yet as mature in HCI as in the other disciplines.

HCI patterns to mature

2.6   Requirements for an Interdisciplinary Pattern Language Framework

With the state of the art in pattern languages in HCI and other disciplines in place, it is time to pose a number of requirements that an interdisciplinary framework based upon pattern languages should fulfil.

Cross-discipline readability. The framework should lead to patterns that are written in a style readable for people from other professions. Those people may be involved in the design process, where their studying the patterns can improve the outcome of a current project, or they may have learning demands. This generally means writing prose instead of shorthand bullet lists, using a minimum of cryptic jargon, and providing understandable examples for nonprofessionals.

Domain-independent, uniform, well-defined format.
The framework should define a consistent overall format for all pattern languages that are created, independent of the domain they address (such as HCI, software engineering, or application domain). Only minor adjustments (such as example media type) should be necessary to cater for the specific needs of each discipline. This format should be specified in a formal way to avoid ambiguous interpretation. (This does not imply that the patterns are written as formulae—see the readability requirement.)

Empirical evidence. The framework should define examples in a pattern as containing published empirical evidence of the validity of the solution where possible.

Domain-appropriate, design-supporting hierarchy. The arrangement that the framework imposes on patterns within each language should lead to a hierarchy that guides a "designer" in the respective domain along the design process in a top-down, unfolding fashion. The arrangement criterion will therefore depend heavily on the domain.

Design dimension coverage. The framework should allow the pattern languages to cover all dimensions, including spatial or temporal configuration, that are relevant to each discipline.

Lifecycle integration. A framework proposing pattern languages as a major work document for interactive system design needs to specify a way in which the languages are to be integrated into a software development lifecycle.

How major existing languages fulfil requirements

Alexander's collection, while fulfilling the requirements of readability and uniform format, do not always give empirical evidence for pattern validity. Their spatial hierarchy is adequate for architecture, though not for other domains, and it does not cover temporal aspects of the artefacts designed. It does, however, offer a good explanation of a design process that uses those patterns.

The collection by Gamma et al. does not fulfil the readability requirement (it is aimed only at developers), but it also has a very uniform format, and gives good empirical evidence. There is, however, not a very supportive hierarchy of the patterns, although they are linked to each other. Using various diagram types, it covers spatial and temporal aspects of a design, but its integration into the lifecycle is not defined; it is rather regarded as a repository to be studied and then used in whatever process model is being used for development.

The collection by Tidwell is quite readable for outsiders, although the format is not quite as uniform, and not all patterns are as elaborate and complete as desired in the above definition. It usually gives empirical evidence, and uses a hierarchy that aligns well with a typical top-down user interface design process. Time and space are covered in the patterns. The use of the language is discussed briefly in the introduction to the collection.

None of the above collections gives a formal definition of pattern structure, nor do they address more than their own single domain.

The following chapter will present an interdisciplinary pattern-based framework for interaction design that aims to fulfil these requirements.

Chapter 3

An Interdisciplinary Pattern Framework

> *"These rules, the semiotic language and*
> *grammar of the game, represent a kind of highly*
> *developed secret language, in which several sciences*
> *and arts, but mathematics and music (respectively*
> *musicology) in particular, participate, and which is*
> *capable of expressing, and relating to each other, the*
> *essence and results of nearly all sciences."*
>
> *—Hermann Hesse,*
> *"The Glass Bead Game (Magister Ludi)"*

This chapter presents the interdisciplinary pattern language framework to capture and express design experience in HCI, software engineering, and the application domain of a software project. The chapter contains a formal hypertext model of design patterns and pattern languages, details the components of each pattern, and discusses how instances of such pattern languages can be used to support design, training, and education in the field of interactive hardware and software systems. For a summary of this approach, see also [Borchers, 2000b].

3.1   A Formal Model of Pattern Languages

Formal definition

To define the components of a pattern language regardless of the problem domain it addresses, we first introduce a formal syntactic notation:

1. A *pattern language* is a directed acyclic graph $PL = (\wp, \Re)$ with nodes $\wp = \{P_1, \ldots, P_n\}$ and edges $\Re = \{R_1, \ldots, R_m\}$.

2. Each node $P \in \wp$ represents a *pattern*.

3. For two nodes $P, Q \in \wp$, we say that P *references* Q if and only if there is a directed edge $R \in \Re$ leading from P to Q.

4. The set of edges pointing away from a node $P \in \wp$ is called its *references*, and the set of edges pointing to it is called its *context*.

5. Each node $P \in \wp$ is itself a set $P = \{n, r, i, p, f_1 \ldots f_i, e_1 \ldots e_j, s, d, \}$ of a name n, ranking r, illustration i, problem p with forces $f_1 \ldots f_i$, examples $e_1 \ldots e_j$, the solution s, and diagram d.

Component meanings

The meaning of the components of this notation is defined next:

- Each *pattern* in the language describes a commonly encountered design problem, and suggests a solution that has proven useful in this situation. The pattern language consists of a number of such patterns for a specific design domain, such as urban architecture.

- For any pattern in the language, the *context edges* leading into it from higher-level patterns represent the design situations in which it can be used, and its *reference edges* show what lower-level patterns can be applied next, after it has been used. This relationship establishes a *hierarchy* within the pattern language. It leads the designer from patterns addressing large-scale design issues, to patterns about small details.

- The *name* of a pattern helps to reference it easily, communicate its central idea quickly, and build a vocabulary.

- The *ranking* shows how valid the pattern author believes this specific pattern is. It helps readers to separate early pattern ideas from trusted and tried, timeless patterns.

- The *illustration* is used to quickly "sensitize" readers to the idea of the pattern, even if they are not professionals (cf. *diagram* below). The choice of media is discussed later in this chapter.

- The *problem* states what the major issue is that the pattern addresses.

- The *forces* further elaborate the problem statement. They are aspects of the design context that need to be optimised. They usually come in pairs that contradict each other.

- The *examples* show existing, real-world situations in which the problem at hand can be (or has been) encountered, and they show how it has been solved, and the forces balanced, in those instances. They are taken from the working practice of the domain that the pattern language addresses.

- The *solution* generalizes from the examples a proven way to balance the forces at hand optimally for the given design context.   It is not prescriptive, but generic so that it can generate a solution when it is applied to concrete problem situations of the form that the context specifies.

- The *diagram* summarizes the main idea of the pattern in a schematic way, concentrating on its main points and leaving out unnecessary detail. This representation is usually preferred over the *illustration* format by people from the profession to quickly grasp an idea. Again, the media choice is discussed further below.

Formal definition: for clarity and computer support only

This formal definition helps to clarify the structure of patterns and pattern languages, and gives a domain-independent description of the structure of a pattern language. It is also useful as a model to implement computerized tools that support authoring or browsing pattern languages.

Real patterns are prose

For actual presentation, however, patterns are not represented as formulae, but rather as written texts, to make them easy to read and understand even for people from other professions. Each part of a pattern, and its connections to other patterns, are usually presented as several paragraphs in the pattern description (see, for example, Alexander et al. [1977], or the example on pp. 14ff.). Other media, such as images, animations, audio recordings, etc., are used to augment the pattern description as described above.

The actual form and contents of those pattern components are described in more detail, and with examples for each of the three disciplines involved, later in this chapter. But first we need an way to integrate the pattern framework into the software and user interface design process.

3.2 Pattern Languages in the Software Lifecycle

Fig. 3.1 shows the general result of the pattern-based approach: three pattern languages that describe HCI, software design, and application domain concepts.

HCI bridges gap

The role of the user interface designer, or human factors expert, becomes that of a relay person, talking on the one hand to the user group to arrive at a user interface design, and communicating the resulting requirements to the software engineering group, to help them in creating a software design.

Responsibility shift

It is remarkable that in traditional projects, those two design products are usually shifted much further to the right:

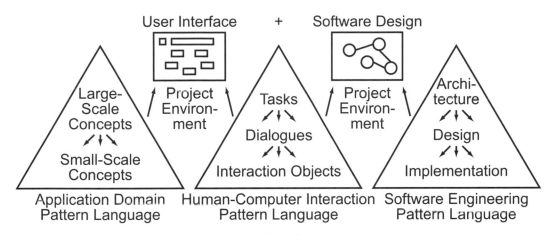

Figure 3.1: Three pattern languages describing application domain, HCI, and software engineering concepts.

software engineers usually create the software design on their own, and often even do the user interface design as part of their job because there is nobody dedicated to this task, and users are hardly involved in the whole process.

The framework suggested in this work shifts those responsibilites further to the left within the diagram: others, especially HCI people, deliver input to the software design, and take over the task of desigining the user interface, with users being able to influence the latter.

Chapter 4 gives an example of this approach. It contains specific instances of the above languages, dealing with the design of interactive exhibits and similar public-access systems. Fig. 3.2 shows those three pattern hierarchies schematically, with a few sample patterns representing each language.

To use the pattern language framework in the process of desiging an interactive software system, it is not mandatory to follow a single fixed design method. As Dix et al. [1998, p. 6] point out:

> "Probably 90% of the value of any interface design technique is that it forces the designer

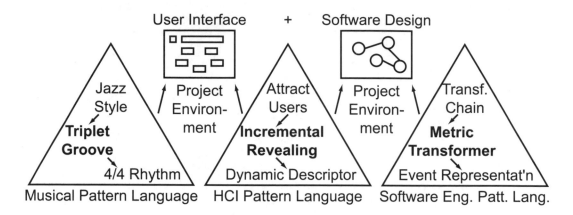

Figure 3.2: Three pattern languages, as they were created for the *WorldBeat* interactive music exhibit.

> to remember that someone (and in particular someone else) will use the system under construction."

However, usability must play a central role in the design process, and this implies that the team must consist of members from different disciplines, including programmers, user interface designers, and end users (see page 3).

The question, then, arises when the pattern concept is to be used within the development process. As with any usability method, there will not be just a single phase of the development cycle dealing with patterns. Instead, patterns will appear at most of the stages of development:

> "Software engineering for interactive system design is not simply a matter of adding one more activity that slots in nicely with the existing activities in the life cycle. Rather, it involves techniques which span the entire life cycle."
> [Dix et al., 1998, p. 179]

3.2.1   The Usability Engineering Lifecycle

To define where pattern languages can be used, we first
need a software life cycle model that is geared towards
usability for interactive system design. The standard waterfall model (see, for example, [Fairley, 1985, p. 38]), orig-
inially devised for the design of large time-sharing systems,
needs to be extended by a model of the usability engineering process of modern interactive systems. Nielsen [1993,
p. 72] proposes the following stages of a *usability engineering
lifecycle* model:

*Waterfall model
insufficient*

1. Know the user

    (a) Individual user characteristics

    (b) The user's current and desired tasks

    (c) Functional analysis

    (d) The evolution of the users and the job

2. Competitive analysis

3. Setting usability goals

    (a) Financial impact analysis

4. Parallel design

5. Participatory design

6. Coordinated design of the total interface

7. Apply guidelines and heuristic analysis

8. Prototyping

9. Empirical testing

10. Iterative design

    (a) Capture design rationale

11. Collect feedback from field use

3.2.2   The Pattern Framework in the Lifecyle

The following paragraphs explain how the three pattern languages of HCI, software engineering, and application domain can be incorporated into the above model of a usability engineering lifecycle.

Patterns for task
analysis

1. Know the user.   The use of pattern languages begins in this first phase: it has to be determined whether the application domain is suitable for expressing its concepts and methods in pattern form. This will be true whenever working in that application domain comprises some sort of creative, designing, or problem-solving activity, because the rules and guidelines that lead people in that application domain in their activity can be formulated as design patterns with the characteristics explained at the beginning of this chapter.

In that case, the analysis of the users' current and desired tasks can use the pattern format to notate those tasks. This can take place in cooperation with the users or domain experts after they have been instructed about the general idea and form of a design pattern. For first-time efforts, those patterns are not required to be perfect in terms of "timeless quality". The pattern format is simply used as a convention for writing down what has to be captured anyway, but with an explicit way of stating forces, alternatives, and connections in those "work patterns".

Another advantage is that this will be the same format in which the HCI and software development patterns are expressed, making all those materials more accessible for the design team, and making it easier for users to recognize their work patterns in the user interface objects and sequences of the product later on.

Patterns generalize
existing solutions

2.   Competitive analysis.   During this phase, existing products in the market are examined to find different solutions to the problems of the product area, and they can be used to do comparative usability evaluation before the own system is being designed. While the internal software architecture is usually not accessible for such systems, and therefore it would be too early to derive software patterns from this examination, HCI pattern languages can generalize successful solutions observed in competing products into a design suggestion for the new system.

3. Setting usability goals.   At this point, the different usability aspects are weighed against each other and prioritized.   These goals, such as learnability, effiency of use, memorability, and low error rate, become the competing forces in high-level HCI patterns that explain how those forces work against each other, and how the design team intends to balance them for this project.   For example, a system used very intensively by highly trained staff will put the balance between memorability and efficiency of use more towards the latter goal, since users who typically access the system daily are less likely to forget about the program's functions.

> HCI pattern forces model design tradeoffs

4. Parallel design.   To explore a larger design space, several initial prototypes of the user interface can be designed by independent teams.   In this case, as well as for later stages, general HCI design patterns (possibly written as books by others outside the team) can take over the role of design guidelines, and help to create a common ground, preserving the usability goals from the last phase, between the design teams working in parallel.

> High-level HCI patterns as guidelines

5. Participatory Design.   Users, also called *application domain experts*, are usually involved in the design process to criticize prototypes, and participate in design discussions. This is the first time that the interdisciplinary value of pattern languages comes into focus: users participating in the design will find it relatively easy to understand the pattern language of their domain, which was established in the first phase (they may even have been actively participating

> Common vocabulary for users and HCI experts

in constructing it). Once they are familiar with the general concept of what a pattern is and what it expresses, this knowledge will help them to understand the set of HCI patterns that the user interface design team has collected and which represents their design values, methods, and guidelines. Conversely, the user interface design team can use the application domain pattern language to talk among themselves and to users about issues of the application domain, in a language that users will find resembling their own terminology. A common vocabulary for users and user interface designers emerges from the combination of both languages.

Vocabulary function

Low-level HCI patterns support consistency

6. Coordinated design of the total interface. The overall goal of coordinated design is to ensure consistency of the resulting interface, including consistency with documentation, help systems and tutorials, but also earlier versions of the product and other products within a company. A vocabulary of HCI design patterns, especially those that address lower-level, concrete design decisions, can help designers communicate more efficiently about their designs, and ensure that the same design concepts are known and respected throughout the interface. Nevertheless, other measures, such as dictionaries of terms used in the user interface, are necessary to support this process of coordination.

HCI patterns as style guides and corporate memory

7. Apply guidelines and heuristic analysis. Style guides, guidelines, and standards are the forms of expressing HCI design experience that are closest to HCI design patterns. Patterns can improve these forms through their structured inclusion of existing examples and an insightful explanation not only of the solution, but also of the problem context in which this solution can be used, and the structured way in which individual patterns are integrated into the hierarchical network of a pattern language, similar to the distinction between general, category-specific, and product-specific guidelines [Nielsen, 1993, p. 93]:

> "Category-specific guidelines … are often a product of corporate memory, to the extent that lessons from previous projects are generalized and made available to future projects. … Product-specific guidelines are often developed as part of individual projects as project members gain a better understanding fof the special usability aspects of their system. Such understanding can be gathered early on through competitive analysis …, and additional insights typically come from user testing of prototypes of the new system."

8. Prototyping. The traditional waterfall model suggests to create actual executable programs only towards the end of the development cycle. Prototypes help to put concrete interfaces into the hands of users much earlier, albeit limited in functionality, scope of features, performance and stability. This aspect of usability engineering is more oriented towards implementation, and here software design patterns play an important role. If the development group can express their architectural standards, components, and specific project ideas in pattern form, then the user interface design group can relate to those concepts more easily, and will better understand the concerns of the development team. For example, the HCI design group could agree to have features in a prototype that are easier to implement without compromising the usefulness of the prototype for testing.

Software patterns inform HCI designers

9. Empirical testing. Prototypes, from initial paper mockups to the final system, are tested with potential users to discover design problems. Application domain patterns can be a resource to construct realistic scenarios for testing. Problems discovered can be related to HCI patterns that could be applied to solve those problems. This is discussed in the next paragraph.

Application domain patterns for test scenarios

Patterns point out
design alternatives

10. Iterative design.   Based upon user feedback, proto-types are redesigned and improved in an iterative process. Patterns of HCI or software design experience are important tools to inform the designers about design options at this point, because they are *constructive*—they suggest how a problem could be solved—, in contrast to general design guidelines, which are mainly *descriptive*, merely stating desirable general features of a "good" finished interactive system.

Of course, all pattern languages used will and should evolve even during the project, to capture the progress in understanding the problem space and improving the design solution. Concrete, successful solutions in the current project can become examples for a given pattern, or warrant the postulation of a new pattern. Subsequent projects will then easily relate to this pattern because it contains examples from a "known" project.

Structural and
process design
rationale

This way, patterns become a very suitable format to capture the design space explored in a project, also called the *structural design rationale*. This post-hoc rationale is an important form of "corporate memory", as it keeps the lessons learned in a project for follow-up projects in a readable, accessible form.

Its counterpart, the *process design rationale*, which documents the good and bad decisions made during design, is less suitable to be documented with patterns since they are defined to capture successful solutions. There is, however, the notion of *anti-patterns*, which document particularly bad solutions that people often implement due to lack of better knowledge. Such patterns, while not patterns in the original sense of the definition, could document alternatives that were discarded during the design process.

Application domain
patterns inform
maintenance and
help desks

11. Collect feedback from field use.   After delivery of a software product, methods such as field tests, follow-up marketing studies, or analysis of helpline calls can be used to see if reality confirms the usability engineering results. In talking to users, the application domain pattern language again plays an important role as a common vocabulary between UI experts and users, and HCI patterns can help to point designers to alternative solutions when problems arise. At the same time, feedback can be used to strengthen the argument of those patterns that created a successful solution, and to rethink those that led to suboptimal results.

This description has shown how the pattern framework can be introduced into the interactive system design process. Next, the form and contents of the various pattern components will be defined in more detail, but first, we need to deal with the notion of time in patterns.

3.3   Time in Patterns

A pattern language is much more than the sum of its individual patterns. The links from patterns addressing large-scale design issues down to small-scale design details help the reader and prospective designer to find the next important pattern as she refines her design. In architecture, the resulting hierarchy is quite simply ordered by geometrical size. Patterns dealing with the general layout of an entire neighbourhood are higher up in the hierarchy than patterns dealing with the question of how to split up an individual house into rooms.

This simple organizing principle ignores one major dimension: time. This works reasonably well for architecture, as the artefacts created (buildings, streets, etc.) do not change themselves substantially over time. Only the events taking place within those environments change over time, and Alexander uses such sequences of events (such as traffic intensity over the course of a day) as a single aspect that influences the design of an environment at the geometric level the pattern addresses.

This approach does not work for HCI, software engineering, and many other application domains, because the artefacts they create do change substantially over time, following the tasks they support. To give a simple example for

Pattern hierarchies need to deal with time

HCI: a railway information kiosk changes from a start page, to a page giving train type options and travel time input fields, to another page displaying possible train connections, etc. In other words, we design user interfaces along a time dimension as well as along two (or three) spatial dimensions.

Therefore, the ordering principle of spatial size has to be expanded into an ordering principle of spatial and temporal expansion. One obvious solution is to put time at the top of the hierarchy, according to the large-scale notion of tasks: In HCI, the designer first thinks about what the complete task looks like, what objects and procedures it contains, and how it can be supported by a series of interactions, or dialogues. Then she goes into detail for each of those steps, designing those shorter dialogues, until each step in the dialogue sequence (or rather graph) is designed with its interaction objects, layout, and spatial geometry.

Other ordering principles are possible, for example those that are more oriented toward the design process itself; these issues were discussed in some detail at the INTERACT'99 workshop [Borchers et al., 2001].

Individual patterns need to deal with time

However, the structure and components of individual patterns also needs to take the temporal dimension into account. This is discussed in the next section.

3.4   Patterns and Their Components in Detail

To ensure that the patterns defined and used within a project actually improve interdisciplinary cooperation, it is important that the characteristics of all patterns follow certain common rules that increase their readability and usefulness for all participants. These characteristics are best explained by looking at the pattern components more closely. For each component, requirements specific to HCI, software engineering, and application domain are also listed.

The Context and References parts are discussed last, since they lead to the question of organizing principles for pattern languages.

For all parts of a pattern, the writing style should avoid genre-specific jargon and notation where possible. If they are necessary, for example, to describe details of a solution, then a generally readable alternative representation should also be included, even if it is less precise.

Avoid jargon

For the same reason—readability—patterns should follow the standard rules of good text design, for example using whole sentences instead of keyword lists.

Whole sentences

3.4.1   Name

Choosing the right name for a pattern is not a trivial task. The name is often the only thing that is remembered literally about a pattern, and it is the pattern part that is referred to most frequently in discussion. In the approach presented here, it becomes a word in the vocabulary for communication between all people involved in the design process, not only from the same but also from other professions.

Vocabulary function

Therefore, the name should express the central idea of the pattern—the core of its solution—as clearly as possible. At the same time, it must remain short enough to be easily remembered. Two words are a common length, four words the maximum.

Alexander [1979, p. 267] gives an example of how his group improved a pattern name over several iterations. The pattern suggests to design the space between street and the front door of a house so that a person experiences a change in the environment and atmosphere while entering the house from the street. From an initial name ENTRY PROCESS (much too vague), via HOUSE STREET RELATIONSHIP (not defining the relationship), and FRONT DOOR INDIRECTLY REACHED FROM STREET (still not defining the place to create), they arrived at a final name that actually captures the

Example: Improving a name

idea that a concrete space, the "transition", needs to be created: ENTRANCE TRANSITION.

To be understandable across disciplines, it is generally better not to choose a name that uses terminology of the domain that is meaningless to outsiders. This is especially true for software engineering patterns, but also HCI patterns. Patterns from the application domain, on the other hand, may use terminology from the application domain to give names to patterns, because one of the goals of that pattern language (see above) is to introduce the designers to this terminology.

For an understandable name, it may help to refer to an analogy from common experience to describe the idea for a pattern. If this analogy is too far-fetched, however, it may become meaningless, or different people may re-map it to the actual problem in different ways, its meaning becoming blurred. As an example, van Welie [2000] called an HCI pattern WHAT'S FOR DINNER?, to refer to the idea of always providing a list of available functions in the current interaction context, but its name may not describe the HCI design solution in an entirely clear way.

3.4.2   Ranking

How invariant is a pattern?

A pattern author will never be equally confident about the validity of all patterns in his collection. It is important to convey this personal rating to the reader, as it can help the latter to decide whether to use a pattern with confidence, or whether it may be worth looking for alternative solutions.

Software engineering, HCI, and application domain patterns should adopt a simple ranking scheme such as the one using zero, one or two stars used in [Alexander et al., 1977] and explained in more detail on page 18.

3.4.3   Illustration

Sensitizing example

The illustration is the first thing—apart from the name—

that a reader encounters when studying a pattern. It has
the important function of *sensitizing* the reader to the problem and solution of the pattern. With the pattern name in
mind, the reader should recognize the situation depicted
in the illustration directly, helping him to understand and
appreciate the values of the solution that the pattern describes. It is an especially accessible representation of the
pattern idea, even for non-professionals.

The choice of media depends on the domain: in archi-   Not always a picture
tecture, Alexander used realistic photos of buildings and
places.

In HCI, it may be necessary to include the notion of time
into the illustration, because, as outlined above, user interfaces often change substantially over the course of an interaction, and this time-dependent behaviour needs to be
expressed as part of those solutions dealing with it. Therefore, an illustration for HCI could simply be a photo of a
user interacting with a system, or a screen shot of a graphical user interface. But where appropriate, it could also be a
short movie showing the behaviour of a user interface over
time, or a different medium for other types of user interfaces (such as an audio recording of someone using a voice-
controlled menu).

In software engineering, it is difficult to show a "real-
world" example of the solution, because the interior design of a software system is not an environment that people
from outside the profession will be familiar with. If the language is mainly used as suggested in this framework—to
support communicating technical aspects of the software
architecture to the user interface designer who has some
understanding of the technical issues—, then it may be
helpful to show sample diagrams of objects interacting in
an existing system, if possible from the application domain
of the project at hand. They will be a concrete instantia-
tion of the abstract concept explained in the pattern (and
sketched in its *diagram* section which is discussed below).

Application domain patterns will usually be much easier
to depict in an illustration. There are always people living

inside this domain—the users—, and their work or other activity practice, and their successful solutions to recurring problems, can be captured, for example, by scenario photographs taken on site, or by other representations of the artefacts created. In music, for example, a short audio recording can introduce the concept that a musical design pattern addresses.

3.4.4 Problem and Forces

Problem more
difficult than solution

It turns out that this part is often the most difficult one to write in a pattern. Expressing exactly what problem a potential pattern solves frequently shows that the problem was not really defined in a sufficiently concrete way. Since patterns should always capture design solutions that balance the various interests in a useful way, it should always be possible to express those conflicting interests as opposing "forces".

The concept of forces is very close to the spatial design solutions of architecture, where one argument, for example, speaks in favour of a higher wall, whereas the other argument supports a lower wall design (see the SITTING WALL pattern on page 16). However, Alexander makes it clear that those forces do not have to be of a purely physical nature. He includes psychological, social, and economical

Force types

forces in his considerations [Alexander, 1979, pp. 108-110].

This idea of forces can be transferred directly to HCI. Spatial forces are at work in geometrical layout considerations, but other forces come from cognitive psychology (such as Gestalt theory [Köhler, 1930, 1992]), and from social and economical issues.

The software engineering field can express many of its design conflicts as opposing forces as well, as has been shown in the software patterns literature. Those forces will usually be of a technical nature. An example is the tradeoff between memory requirements and execution speed of a software system, but also the tradeoff between initial simplicity and flexibility of a software architecture later on.

The existing efforts that have been presented in section 2.4 to carry the pattern idea over to the application domain often fail at expressing their problems using opposing forces. This usually indicates that the solutions presented are not really design-oriented patterns balancing conflicting design goals, but rather *activity patterns* that just describe existing work practice without validating it. This is one of the reasons why the present framework requires that the application domain has to incorporate some kind of creative, problem-solving, or designing work activity. Otherwise it may not be possible to put its concepts into pattern form, and other techniques may be more applicable to model the application domain.

3.4.5   Examples

The examples are vital to a pattern for two reasons. First, they serve to lead the novice reader towards the general solution of the pattern via a set of concrete, existing instantiations of this solution. Second, they give the professional reader empirical, verifiable evidence of the validity of the pattern.

Examples are introduction and proof

To make a pattern as understandable as possible, it is better to use an inductive than a deductive style. This means that the concrete examples are presented first, and then generalized into the solution. They should refer to existing systems that are as widely known as possible, and explain how those systems solve the problem described before. Additional illustrations should be used where available.

Inductive approach

In HCI, because of its closeness to architecture, it is relatively easy to describe examples that the reader can relate to. For example, to explain the idea of dynamic information appearing close to an object upon request, features of common desktop operating systems, such as Mac OS® Balloon Help, or Microsoft Windows® Tool Tips, can be shown. Since people from outside HCI design have usually interacted with such systems as well, they are usually able to understand those examples and see the common solution in them that leads them to the core of the pattern.

For software engineering, it may be easy to come up with existing systems that use a certain design solution, but it will be more difficult to make those examples understandable to people from outside the profession, since architectural details are usually not directly "visible" in an interactive software system, but rather indirectly influence external characteristics such as performance, stability, or flexibility. Nevertheless, as with the opening illustration, it should usually be possible to show examples that are understandable to HCI people with some computing expertise.

In the application domain, the examples are drawn from work practice or artefacts created, and help to underline the importance of the application domain patterns they exemplify to the remaining design team.

3.4.6   Solution

Solution generalizes examples

This is the central message of each pattern. It takes the lessons to be learned from the examples, and generalizes them into a constructive design recommendation that can be applied in varying situations whenever a problem is encountered as described in the context.

In HCI, those solutions deal with the user interface design of interactive systems. They describe psychological, spatial and temporal rules and configurations that create a more intuitive user experience, making the interaction as natural and simple as possible and appropriate for the application domain.

In software engineering, the solutions give design recommendations for the internals of the software system, from global, architectural issues down to implementation details. They aim at improving the resulting system performance with respect to the tasks it is to support.

In the application domain, the solution describes the way problems are solved in the work practice or other activity that the software system is going to support. They can serve as starting point for the way the software solves those problems, with the possibility of improving upon those practices through the introduction of the system.

In any case, the solution should be put into a succinct form (usually not more than a few short sentences). It is something that is often read after glancing at a pattern, to find out what the core message of the pattern is.

3.4.7 Diagram

The *diagram* summarizes the main idea of the pattern in a schematic way, concentrating on its main points and leaving out unnecessary detail. It is more concise and schematic than the *illustration*.

Diagram: concise schematic for professionals

The medium used depends on the pattern language domain: For architecture, the medium chosen by Alexander is a graphical sketch. In HCI, the graphical sketch can capture spatial designs, and a storyboard sketch can deal with temporal design aspects.

Not always graphical

In software engineering, UML diagrams or even pseudo-code may express the pattern idea very precisely, and similar forms are used, for example, in [Gamma et al., 1995]. However, when choosing a notation, it has to be kept in mind that this notation also needs to be sufficiently readable and accessible for readers from outside the profession.

In the application domain, the choice depends on the nature of that domain. Most domains have some form of shorthand notation to express their concepts. In music, for example, this shorthand is the musical score notation.

3.4.8 Context and References

The *context*, together with the *references*, represents the added value that turns a loose collection of patterns into a pattern language. Once a reader has decided to apply a

Context and references make a pattern language

pattern, its references should point her to other, "smaller" patterns that can be applied next to refine the design further. The context is the "inverse function" of the references, and sets the stage for the reader to make it clear when the current pattern can be applied.

Pattern hierarchy according to "size"

The above notion of pattern "size" as organizing principle works very well in architecture, where patterns can be sorted into a hierarchy according to the size of the space they apply to. A pattern describing how to layout an entire neighbourhood is "larger" than a pattern dealing with the placement of windows in a single room. Alexander used this organizing principle because it reflects the order in which he suggests to carry out the design: initial designs create a broad layout, which is then *refined* by subsequently applying smaller design patterns.

HCI actually uses a similar design sequence with time as an added dimension, especially when following the ideas of user-centred design and iterative prototyping as outlined in the usability engineering lifecycle: after task analysis, which in the pattern framework creates the application domain pattern language, the user interface is designed in an iterative process. The first designs are crude prototypes, paper sketches, or storyboards that deal with the overall structure of the interaction. Only in subsequent iterations, those designs are refined, user interface objects identified, until final prototypes deal with small-scale issues of graphical layout etc. (Of course, this does not imply that those small-scale patterns are less important, because the overall "Quality Without a Name" of the system depends on the successful combination of patterns at all levels.)

In software engineering, the design process is again similar if a top-down process is employed. In this case, considerations about the total system architecture lead to questions about groups of interacting components, down to implementation details of individual software classes or modules. Of course, this does not mean that no implementation takes place until the end of the design cycle (that would imply going back to the waterfall model). Instead, it indicates that the technical quality of the implementation does not need to be optimized for the first software prototypes, and that patterns to improve that quality can be applied later in the software development process.

This concludes the pattern-based framework for interaction design. The next chapter shows sample pattern languages from this approach. In particular, the HCI pattern language should be useful to many readers in its own right.

Chapter 4

A Pattern Language for Interactive Music Exhibits

"Der Worte sind genug gewechselt,
Laßt mich auch endlich Taten sehn!"

—*J. W. von Goethe: Faust*

This chapter shows an example of the pattern approach to interaction design, and therefore contains three pattern languages.

Three pattern languages, drawn from several projects.

The structure of these patterns follows the formal definition given in section 3.1, and the component type descriptions presented in section 3.4.

Structure follows formal definition

To present patterns, Alexander [1979] has established a set of typographical rules that make the structure of patterns visible without requiring explicit text labels. This improves readability of the pattern text, and is in line with well-known design guidelines against excessive labeling [Norman, 1988].

Structuring through typography

Therefore, the pattern languages in this chapter are formatted in a way that very closely follows these typographical

rules used by Alexander [1979]. The rules have been identified and discussed in detail in section 2.3.

The patterns in this chapter represent the experience that
the author has gathered in managing the development of
the following interactive exhibits, or *actibits,* and designing
their user interface:

WorldBeat

1. In the *WorldBeat* project, an award-winning interactive exhibit about computers and music was created
   for permanent display in the *Ars Electronica Center*, a
   technology and art museum and venue centre in Linz,
   Austria. Since many of the patterns reference this system as an example, it is described in more detail in
   chapter 5.

Interactive Fugue

2. In the *Interactive Fugue* project, an interactive exhibit
   was designed to teach basic facts about the classical
   musical form of the Fugue, as used by composer Johann Sebastian Bach. The system was implemented
   and tested with some users, although it has not yet
   been permanently installed as a public exhibit.

Personal Orchestra

3. In the *Personal Orchestra* project, a system was designed and implemented that allows users to conduct
   various recorded audio and video performances of
   the Vienna Philharmonic Orchestra, controlling the
   orchestra's tempo and dynamics in real time. The system is on permanent display in the HOUSE OF MUSIC
   VIENNA, a newly opened major museum and exhibition centre in Vienna.

Virtual Vienna

4. In the *Virtual Vienna* project, a virtual city tour of Vienna was designed and implemented that leads visitors to music-historically important places throughout Austria's capital. This system will also become a
   permanent exhibit in the aforementioned HOUSE OF
   MUSIC VIENNA.

Of course, the patterns also contain references to many
other sources to strengthen the validity of each pattern.

Since user-centred design of interactive systems starts with learning about the application domain of a system, the first of the three pattern languages is about this application domain, "music".

Naturally, it does not cover all existing musical styles. Instead, it is the pattern language of all those musical concepts that were used in the first system, *WorldBeat*, particularly in those parts that deal with blues as musical style. It shows how some basic, but important aspects of the musical knowledge of an experienced blues player can be captured in pattern form.

Application domain: pattern language for blues music

The second pattern language leads from domain and task analysis to interaction design. As it is central to this text, it is the largest of the three languages. It is about HCI, and describes successful solutions to user interface design problems for interactive exhibits, as applied in the various systems listed above.

HCI: pattern language for interactive exhibits

The third pattern language is about software design solutions for such systems. It reports successful solutions in software architecture, software design, and implementation that we used in the various projects.

Software eng.: pattern language for interactive music software

The languages may seem to be useful only for a very specific area, and indeed they will be of most use for designers of similar systems. The user interface design patterns, however, address interactive exhibits of any kind, not only those dealing with music as their subject area.

Moreover, the recent success of desktop software designed in a much more playful, exhibit-like form than standard applications shows that the guidelines for exhibit design are a very good starting point to create software for other entertainment and work situations. An example of this new type of software is *Kai's Power Show* (see Fig. 4.1).

HCI patterns useful for kiosks and desktop software

For all three languages, the best way to get a quick overview is to have a look at the *pattern language graph* at the beginning of each language. It shows the names of all patterns in that language, and their interconnection through context/reference links.

Pattern graphs

Figure 4.1: *Kai's Power Show,* an application for presentation authoring with an exhibit-like interface.

4.1 Musical Pattern Language

This pattern language describes those important principles of the musical style *blues* that are used in the *WorldBeat* improvisation component. An overview of this language is shown in Fig. 4.2. As with all pattern languages, the patterns are sorted so that the reader is guided from large-scale to small-scale principles. In addition, the patterns of this language are arranged from left to right into groups addressing harmonic, melodic, and rhythmical aspects of a piece.

As explained in the last chapter, the application domain is seen as a design domain, making the uniform pattern format suitable for expressing knowledge in that domain. In this case, the task of composing or (more suitably) improvising a blues piece is considered a design activity, creating the music as a result. Even though the actual performing activity will not follow an elaborate, top-down design pro-

cess, learning how to play blues is simplified by this structuring into a pattern hierarchy.

Naturally, not all the rules and principles used in blues improvisation are included, but only those that were required
for the musical model used in the exhibit. For example, the
entire area of vocal performance, where patterns in blues
lyrics such as REPEATED TWO-LINERS could be identified,
has been left out because it is not addressed in the World-
Beat improvisation component either. Similarly, basic music patterns unspecific to blues, such as the underlying 4/4
RHYTHM or CHROMATIC SCALE, are not included because
their concepts are also assumed as given in the exhibit.

Only patterns useful
for exhibit included

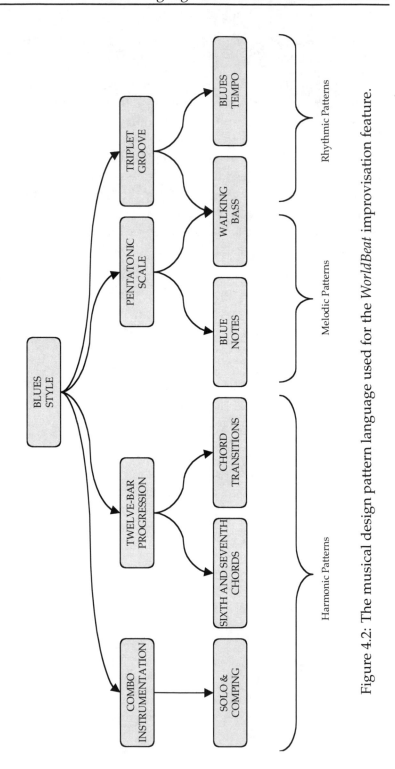

Figure 4.2: The musical design pattern language used for the *WorldBeat* improvisation feature.

M1 BLUES STYLE

Figure 4.3: Railroad workers.

... you are searching for a musical style to play, sing, and improvise in, probably together with other players, without having formally rehearsed anything together.

◇◇◇

Playing together with others without prior rehearsal is often desirable on spontaneous occasions. But without a common repertoire of defined pieces, it is hard to play well together.

The opening photograph shows a group of Afro-American railroad workers. Such working situations created the desire to sing together to ease the workload and coordinate the work. Spiritual events were another source for spontaneous group music. The resulting music was shaped by the African cultural roots of many American slaves, with syncopated beats and pentatonic melodies.

Work song

Since jazz has become a mainstream musical style, jazz musicians invariably know the blues style as the root of the entire domain of jazz music. At spontaneous meetings and "jam sessions", a blues is often chosen to start playing together, or when no sheet music is available and no pieces

Jam sessions

are known by all players. Despite its simple structure, it can create very emotional and appealing performances.

Therefore:

Use the *blues* style to start playing together with others. Make sure that its simple basic harmonic form is known by everybody, and agree on tempo, key choice, choruses, and introduction and endings. With that in place, you can start playing immediately, and still create a coherent musical impression.

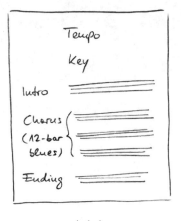

◇◇◇

Choose a suitable set of instruments in your group— COMBO INSTRUMENTATION (M2). Use the basic blues progression or an extension of it—TWELVE-BAR PROGRES- SION (M4). For improvisation, start with the pentatonic note scale as note material—PENTATONIC SCALE (M7), and make sure everybody knows about the characteristic, swinging playing style—TRIPLET GROOVE (M9). . . .

M2   COMBO INSTRUMENTATION

Figure 4.4: Louis Armstrong's *Hot Five:* a jazz combo.

. . . you wish to play a blues piece—BLUES STYLE (M1). First, you need to see what instruments will be played together.

◇◇◇

Too many instruments, especially with unrehearsed performance, tend to sound too dense. On the other hand, too few instruments may mean that vital harmonic, rhythmic, or melodic parts are not played by anyone.

Early blues music was played using very simple means: vocals and hand-clapping often were enough.

Today, a variety of instruments is used, but some, such as drums and bass, have become standard for rhythmic accompaniment, and instruments such as guitar or piano often add the harmonic information to a piece. Solo instruments such as trumpet, saxophone, etc. take over the role of the vocalist, adding the melodic dimension. However, most combos combine some instruments from the rhythmic/harmonic section with some from the melodic section to create a balanced musical spectrum.

From vocals and hand-clapping, to rhythm and solo instruments

Therefore:

Use a combination of one or several rhythm section instruments, such as drums, bass, piano, or guitar, plus one or several solo instruments, such as vocals, harmonica, trumpet, or saxophone.

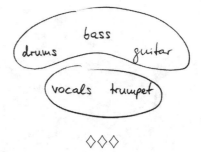

◇◇◇

See that the combo takes turns in improvising—SOLO & COMPING (M3). . . .

M3   SOLO & COMPING *

Figure 4.5: Jimmy Garrison accompanying John Coltrane.

...you have decided on a combination of instruments for your performance—COMBO INSTRUMENTATION (M2). Now you have to decide when each instrument plays which role in the performance.

Improvisation is the key to good blues music, however players need to agree on a "protocol" to avoid a too dense and chaotic musical outcome, where all players solo all the time.

In contrast to symphonic compositions, most blues and jazz performances divide players into the roles of soloist and accompanying ("comping") players. These roles usually change dynamically during a piece.

Comping

Recordings from classic jazz combos often reveal a structure where the melody ("head") of a piece is played first, followed by all players taking turns to improvise over this theme, and completed by a repetition of the head to end the performance.

Therefore:

Let players take turns in soloing, including melody instruments as well as accompanying instruments. The remaining players step back musically, and some of them accompany the soloist. Each soloist signals the next soloist when he is finished.

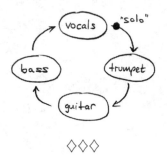

◇◇◇

This is a basic pattern that has no further references within this pattern language.

M4   TWELVE-BAR PROGRESSION *

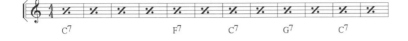

Figure 4.6: Chord progression for a twelve-bar blues.

. . . you wish to play some blues music—BLUES STYLE (M1). An important choice to make is the sequence, or *progression* of chords to play.

◇◇◇

blues depends on improvisation, and should therefore be interpreted as freely as possible, but there is a basic harmonic structure that the players need to know in order to make their piece sound like blues music.

Miller [1978, p. 42] defines the blues harmony as consisting of three 4-bar groups: four bars tonic (I)[1]; two bars subdominant plus two bars tonic; two bars dominant plus two bars tonic, He also explains that this is just the most frequent form, and that deviations are quite common.

Three 4-bar groups

Countless blues recordings reflect this basic harmonic structure, and it has carried over to later music as well— for example, the choruses in Bill Hailey's well-known *Rock Around The Clock*.

Therefore:

Use the simple twelve-bar blues progression as the basic harmonic form of each chorus: four bars tonic—two bars subdominant plus two bars tonic—two bars dominant plus two bars tonic.

---

[1]In music, the key of a piece, or part of a piece, is referred to as the tonic, or first degree, and referenced by a roman I. Other keys are referenced in relation to this key, so in a C major piece, I = C, IV = F, V = G, etc. This standard musical notation is used throughout the following examples.

| I | I | I | I |

| IV | IV | I | I |

| V | V | I | I |

◇◇◇

Each musical degree in the above progression typically consists of a dominant sixth or seventh chord—SIXTH AND SEVENTH CHORDS (M5). The simple progression can be extended with inserted transitions to other chords—CHORD TRANSITIONS (M6). ...

M5   SIXTH AND SEVENTH CHORDS

Figure 4.7: Progression with alternating sixth chords.

…as overall structure, you have agreed upon a certain sequence of chords for your performance—TWELVE-BAR PROGRESSION (M4). Now you need to decide how to fine-structure that progression.

◇◇◇

To create a well-sounding blues piece, you have to stay within the chord structure you have agreed on, but the basic chords of the progression sound simplistic if they are not enriched in any way.

A typical left-hand piano accompaniment for blues music, as shown in the opening picture, uses quarter-note chords that change between including the fifth and sixth step, effectively changing the base chord into a sixth chord every other beat.

Left-hand piano accompaniment

Blues, like many other musical styles, also often uses minor seventh chords when the current chord is in a dominant function (leading a fifth backwards) to the next chord, such as a G^7 before a C major chord.

Dominant seventh chords

Therefore:

Instead of the simple triad chords from the progression, frequently use sixth chords, and use seventh chords if you are about to step back a fifth to the next chord.

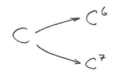

◇◇◇

This is a basic pattern that has no further references within this pattern language.

M6   CHORD TRANSITIONS

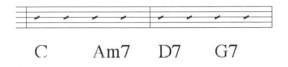

C   Am7   D7   G7

Figure 4.8: I–VI–II–V chord transition.

…you have found a basic harmonic structure—TWELVE-BAR PROGRESSION (M4). Now you need to decide if you wish to refine and extend it beyond its basic form.

◇◇◇

The twelve-bar schema is important to create a piece that sounds like blues, but without changing the schema, pieces will sound very similar.

A technique used very frequently to vary chord sequences is to replace a chord by a transition leading to the following chord via a series of fifth intervals. For example, the last two tonic bars in the twelve-bar progression are often replaced by a sequence such as "I-VI-II-V", lasting half a bar each and leading back to the tonic (I) of the next chorus via a series of downward steps through the fifth circle.

II-V-I progression

Therefore:

Replace parts of the twelve-bar progression with more complex chord sequences to create a more complex musical style. Concentrate on replacing chords at the end of each four-bar group, and frequently use a transition that leads back to the following chord via a sequence of fifth steps.

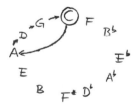

◇◇◇

This is a basic pattern that has no further references within this pattern language.

M7   PENTATONIC SCALE **

Figure 4.9: *Nice Work If You Can Get It.*

...you want to improvise over a blues piece—BLUES STYLE (M1), so you now want to know which notes in the current key are especially useful as "raw material" for improvisation.

◇◇◇

Just using the notes of the simple triad chords of the current key is too simple for improvisation. But using all notes in the chromatic scale equally would remove the harmonic context completely.

Most western music is based on the chromatic scale, but uses only a subset of it as material for creating melodies. The remaining note of the scale are used as well, but less frequently and with less emphasis.

Blues music has its roots in African music, where *pentatonic scales* are the most frequently used [Binkowski, 1988, p. 130]. For example, a C major pentatonic scale contains the five notes C, D, E, G, and A. It contains no semitone steps, which makes it fit well with a wide range of chords.

African music scales

The opening example shows the refrain of the jazz standard "Nice Work If You Can Get It". Note that the melody only uses the notes G, A, B, D, and E, which is exactly the pentatonic scale over the base key of this piece, G major.

Therefore:

Use a scale containing the prime, second, third, fifth and sixth note of the major scale in the current chord as your preferred note material for improvisation.

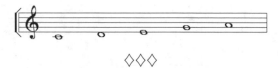

◇◇◇

The pentatonic scale is also a good starting point to play a bass line—WALKING BASS (M10). For a genuine blues sound, you need to extend the pentatonic scale with additional "blue" notes—BLUE NOTES (M8). . . .

M8   BLUE NOTES **

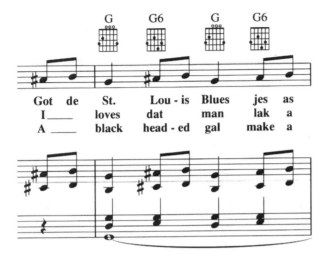

Figure 4.10: *St. Louis Blues.*

...you are thinking about the melodic material for blues improvisation—PENTATONIC SCALE (M7), and you now want to extend the basic note material.

◇◇◇

The pure pentatonic scale does not create enough musical tension for a blues piece. But not all other notes can be used to enrich the scale; additional notes have to support the musical impression typical of blues style music.

African music, as the root of blues, enriches the pentatonic scale with notes that have no direct correspondence in the chromatic scale [Binkowski, 1988, p. 171]: they lie between the flat and natural notes of the third, fifth, and seventh degree. To western listeners, the resulting scale sounds similar to a minor scale, creating a musical impression of sadness or feeling "blue", which gave the blues its name.

Blue notes outside chromatic scale

Many instruments used in jazz and blues, such as vocal, bass, and guitar, can produce those notes outside the chromatic scale; other instruments approximate them, usually using the lower of the two neighbouring chromatic pitches. The notes are often slid up towards the next natural note.

Sliding

Therefore:

Use the pitches between flat and natural third, flat and natural fifth, and flat and natural seventh of your current scale as *blue notes***, in addition to the pentatonic scale material. If your instrument can only play chromatic notes, use both notes, frequently sliding from the lower to the upper note.**

◇◇◇

This is a basic pattern that has no further references within this pattern language.

M9 TRIPLET GROOVE **

Figure 4.11: *Lover Man.*

...you wish to play a blues style piece—BLUES STYLE (M1). You should use a certain rhythmic feeling when playing, which is particular to jazz music in general.

◇◇◇

Players need to create a swinging rhythmic feeling. The straight rhythm from other musical styles does not create this effect. At the same time, sheet music cannot include all rhythmic variances, because it would become too complex and unreadable.

Most jazz recordings show the solution to this problem. It is an often triplet shift of the intermediate beat in the rhythm section of a band to make the music "swing". For example, if the drummer's score contains a sequence of eighth notes to play on his hi-hat, he will interpret them roughly as an alternating sequence of 2+1 triplet eighth notes to create the swing feeling. Comparative studies of jazz recordings show that most bands actually have their own specific groove timing that helps us recognize them.

Triple shifts make music swing

Therefore:

Where the written music contains an evenly spaced pattern of eighth notes, shift every second eighth note in the pattern backwards in time by about one third of its length, shortening it accordingly, and make the preceding

eighth note one third longer. **Instead of a rhythmic length ratio of 1:1, the resulting pattern are alternating notes with a length ratio of $\frac{2}{3}$: $\frac{1}{3}$. Two straight eighth notes have been changed into 2+1 triplet eighth notes. This rhythmic shift creates what musicians call the "laid-back groove" in a performed piece. The actual shift percentage can vary widely, but usually depends on the tempo: the faster a piece is, the less shifting takes place.**

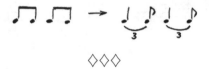

◇◇◇

The bass line can occasionally pick up this groove to make its standard bass pattern more varied—WALKING BASS (M10). For blues music, the rhythmic shift should even more than a triplet, because of the slow tempo—BLUES TEMPO (M11). ...

M10   WALKING BASS *

Figure 4.12: A walking bass line.

... you want to play blues–BLUES STYLE (M1), and you now need to find a suitable bass line for the music.

◇◇◇

The bass needs more note material than what is included in the current harmony chord. But adding arbitrary notes with large intervals between them leads to a loss of continuity and harmonic context in the music perceived.

A standard bass line used frequently in blues and boogie pieces consists of quarter notes that walk up and down a scale of the first, third, fifth, sixth, and minor seventh degree in the current harmony. It is the most frequently used walking bass line, but can be varied to become more interesting, and to cover other harmonic progressions, as shown in the opening picture: as long as the line uses quarter notes continuously, with the chord root appearing at the beginning of each new chord, the last quarter before a chord change leading to the next chord root, and other notes from the chord for any notes in between, a suitable accompaniment with a "walking" impression is created [Akkerman, 2000].

Bass lines that "walk"

Therefore:

On the first beat of a new chord, play the chord root. On the following beats, play other notes from the chord, such as the third, fifth, sixth, or seventh, depending on the chord symbol. On the last beat before a chord change, however, play a note approaching the next chord root from a half-step above or below.

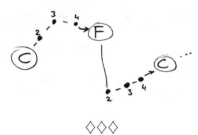

◇◇◇

This is a basic pattern that has no further references within this pattern language.

M11 BLUES TEMPO

Figure 4.13: *Everyday I Have The Blues.*

... you have found a way to accompany your blues piece—
WALKING BASS (M10). You now have to agree on a tempo.

◇◇◇

**Blues needs a certain laziness to create the right mood,
however, if the tempo is too slow, the music can use its
rhythmic continuity and drive.**

Typical blues recordings have a tempo of around 60–120
beats per minute (bpm). For example, Spencer Williams'
classic *Basin Street Blues* is played at around 100 bpm. The
opening example also suggests a "walking blues" tempo.

60–120 bpm

Therefore:

**Choose a tempo between 48 for a very slow blues, and 128
for a fast, rhythm-and-blues piece.**

◇◇◇

This is a basic pattern that has no further references within
this pattern language.

4.2 HCI Pattern Language

Public interactive
systems

This section presents a language of design patterns for
human–computer interaction. They address the task of designing interactive systems that are used in public spaces.
This scenario requires designers to pay special consideration to the immediate usability of their systems. They need
to design for a target group who are typically first-time and
one-time users at the same time, and who generally have no
professional motivation requiring them to use the system.
Overall interaction duration is often within a few minutes
only.

Kiosk system
classification

Typical systems falling into this category include interactive exhibits at museums and exhibition centres, but also
other public systems that are generally referred to as *kiosk
systems*. These systems can be classified into four groups,
according to their main function [Borchers et al., 1995]:

Information Kiosks have the primary goal to provide information in a usually limited subject field. An example is an interactive train schedule information system at a railway station.

Advertising Kiosks that are installed to present a company or institution or its products and services to the
public. Today, the web presence of many companies
still falls into this class.

Service Kiosks emphasize the flow of information from
the user back to the system—for example, hotel reser-
vation systems.

Entertainment Kiosks may just help people pass their
time, or serve to attract customers for a business.
However, they often have a secondary function of one
of the other kiosk types.

Of course, real systems will often belong to two or more of
the above classes, but there is usually a primary goal that

should be identified for the system as a whole, or at least for its individual content parts.

The systems that are used as primary source for examples in the following patterns belong to the class of interactive exhibits. They can be classified as entertainment kiosks that have an educational message to be delivered, but which is wrapped into an engaging interactive experience.

Interactive exhibits

The hierarchy of patterns is presented in Fig. 4.14, followed by the individual patterns themselves.

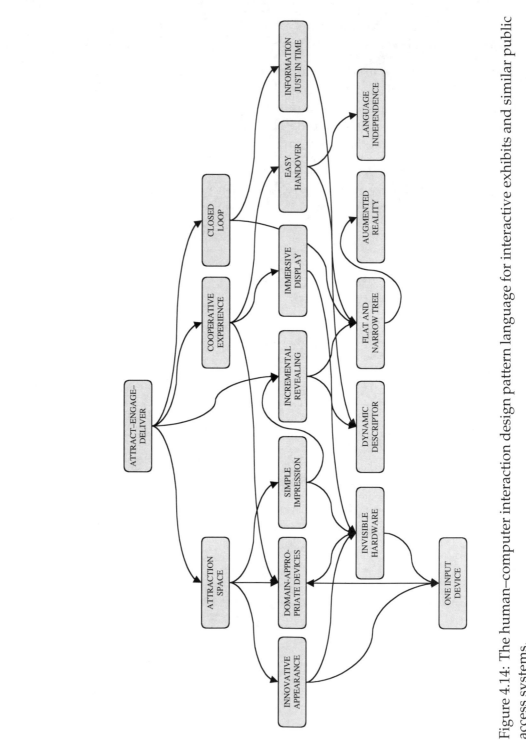

Figure 4.14: The human–computer interaction design pattern language for interactive exhibits and similar public access systems.

H1 ATTRACT–ENGAGE–DELIVER *

Figure 4.15: Visitors in the Ars Electronica Center.

...the prerequisites for interaction design, such as initial user profiling and task analysis, are fulfilled, and you are now starting to design the overall user experience of your interactive exhibit. You want to decide what the goal of the interaction is, and what interaction phases can be distinguished to achieve that goal.

◇◇◇

An interactive exhibit is mostly used by people for entertainment, but it usually has to fulfil a purpose beyond that. However, the intended usage duration is generally limited because many visitors should be able to experience the exhibit over the course of a day.

The user profile of an interactive exhibit is usually very broad, and users generally have no strong need to use such a system. This means that the initial interest to use such a system must be motivated by the system itself.

Most interactive exhibits, however, are not just for entertainment. Their goal is deliver a "message"—to explain

Delivering a message

some facts, concepts, or ideas—to the user, through the interaction. Therefore, it is important, after the initial attraction, to keep the user occupied until this message can be delivered.

But once this goal has been achieved, it is important to allow the user to end the session in a planned and positive way. Users generally should not break off in the middle of an interaction because they have become bored, or because they do not know when they will be able to leave the system orderly.

Exploratorium

For example, in the *Exploratorium*, a children's technology discovery museum in San Francisco, each exhibit is labelled with a three-sentence description of the following form:

To do and notice: This part explains briefly what to do with the exhibit, which buttons to push or levers to move, and what to look for in the system reaction. For example, an exhibit on glass fibres would tell the user to press a button to light a lamp, and to observe how the light comes out of the end of a bent glass fibre.

What's going on? The second sentence summarizes what is happening in the system. In the example, it would explain how the light is reflected by the inside of the glass fibre wall.

So What? The last sentence, probably most important, tells the visitor why this phenomenon is important. In the example, it would explain how glass fibre cables can be used to transmit information very quickly.

These descriptions actually make the attraction, engaging, and delivering phases of the interaction with an exhibit explicit.

WorldBeat: Explore features

Similarly, the *WorldBeat* system wants to convey an overall message: that computers open up new ways to interact with music. Each of the various sub-functions of the

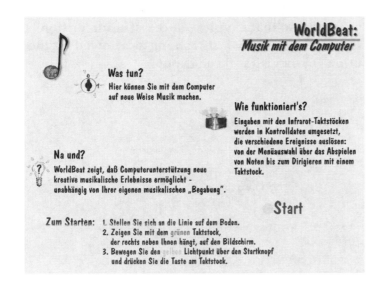

Figure 4.16: The *WorldBeat* start screen, explaining what to do, how the system works, and what its main message is.

system shows a more specific example of this general message: how computers can help with conducting, improvising, finding music, etc. The system initially attracts visitors with an interesting yet simple interface that quickly leads to a main selection display of those features. Each feature in turn briefly and explicitly explains what its "message" is. When the user has explored one of those features, he has taken its specific message with him, and is returned to the main selection page where he can continue exploring the system, or leave the exhibit in a consistent and satisfying way. Nobody explores the system completely; this would also take much longer than the interaction duration as planned by the exhibition centre. Instead, most users explore only a few of the features, but still take the messages from those features with them.

Therefore:

Design the interaction so that it takes place in three phases: attracting users, engaging them, and delivering one of the "messages" to them which the system wants to convey. Attach an average interaction time to each of

those phases so that a typical, successful interaction with message delivery only lasts as long as allowed by the institution for its visitor throughput.

◇◇◇

To get people to have a closer look at your system in the first place, attract them with the initial appearance of your system when they are close to it—ATTRACTION SPACE (H2). To keep them engaged, gradually reveal more interesting features of your system to them—INCREMENTAL REVEALING (H6). If your system has several messages to convey, let the user know when each one is delivered, and offer an option to leave the system—CLOSED LOOP (H9). ...

H2   ATTRACTION SPACE *

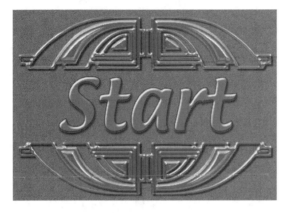

Figure 4.17: Sample start button design.

... you are designing the interactive appearance of an interactive exhibit—ATTRACT–ENGAGE–DELIVER (H1). You are currently looking at the first step, and need to find out what the system should look like when it is first encountered by the user, and how it can fit into its environment.

◇◇◇

In an environment such as an exhibition centre, many systems are competing for the visitor's attention. To find out about a system's message, visitors first have to notice it. However, if a system is too visually active or noisy in its appearance, it can disturb the atmosphere of its entire environment.

When an interactive system is not being used, its appearance in the "idle" state is the first thing that a passing visitor notices. If this impression does not draw the visitor towards the exhibit, he will never find out about what the system has to offer. After all, there is usually nothing that forces a visitor to use any of the stations in an exhibition centre. This is very different from the situation in which, for example, office software is used: there, users need to get a job done, and have their own initial motivation to approach and explore the system.

Idle state

Visual and auditory
channels

There are two principal channels that an exhibit can use to increase its noticeability: visual signals, which are directed and therefore only noticed if the visitor looks into that direction, and auditory signals, which are undirected and therefore much stronger, since they are noticed by everybody in the vicinity. Strong visual cues such as intensive animation or very large displays can also have an undirected effect, since they draw attention even when they are observed in the visual periphery of the user.

However, a system must not create too much audible noise or visual disturbance, because a sensory "overflow" will irritate users and make them leave the entire environment to escape from such a multimedia chaos. Instead, the systems within such an environment need to coexist to create a positive overall experience for the visitor.

WorldBeat: Visual
attraction

The *WorldBeat* exhibit (see appendix B) solves this conflict in the following way. Although it is an exhibit about music, it does not create any noise when not in use. Instead, it shows a very simple, and aesthetically pleasing, opening screen that invites the visitor to explore the exhibit. No animation is used, and the impression is quite calm. But its main attraction is created by a different visual cue: a pair of infrared batons is dangling from the ceiling in front of the screen. There is a little light blinking on each baton, barely visible, but just enough to show that the batons are "alive". These batons look interesting, they are something the user has never seen before, and therefore invite exploration. Despite this attractive appearance, the exhibit does not dominate the space around it further than its distance to the next exhibit allows, neither by auditory nor visual means.

Start button

Another example is a typical start screen of a video game or kiosk system. These screens often use a specially rendered, three-dimensional, or textured "Start" button (see the opening picture) that the user has to press to enter the system. This button looks much more inviting than the simple word "Start" on a screen, but it also only dominates the space belonging to the display of this particular system.

Naturally, the right level of sensory stimulation depends

on the application domain. A video games arcade hall is a good example of this point. It often creates a noisy environment with flashing light effects, where the stimuli from neighbouring systems strongly interfere. While this is the environment many players seem to like; it is obvious that it would be far too overloaded to be adequate for studying exhibits in an exposition centre.

In 1998, the *Techniek Museum Delft* created an exhibition called "De Digitale Schoolreis" (The Digital Class Excursion), which included, among other exhibits, a dolphin "Fin-Fin" (an interactive computer character) that children could interact with. The fact, however, that this dolphin started whistling every few minutes to attract attention to itself soon drove the museum staff crazy; it penetrated the attraction space of an entire floor. This shows that especially audio stimuli can easily become a nuisance, not only in office software, but also in interactive exhibits.

Fin-Fin

Therefore:

Define an attraction space around your system that is as large as possible, but without penetrating the attraction spaces of neighbouring exhibits. Then, make sure that your system does not frequently violate this border. To achieve this, use primarily static visual stimuli in the physical shape and appearance of your interface that look attractive by their design alone. Avoid excessive animation, and especially frequent undirected stimuli such as audio, because they easily interfere with neighbouring attraction spaces.

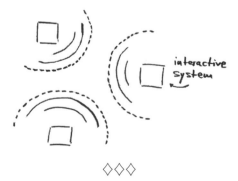

◇◇◇

A good way to attract people is to make your system look like something they have never seen before—INNOVATIVE APPEARANCE (H12). However, you should make sure that your system does not scare off potential users because it looks too complicated to use—SIMPLE IMPRESSION (H5). You can convey a quick first idea of what your system is about by using periphery that matches your application area—DOMAIN-APPROPRIATE DEVICES (H11). . . .

H3 COOPERATIVE EXPERIENCE **

Figure 4.18: Two museum visitors using *WorldBeat* together.

. . . the overall structure of the interaction is in place—
ATTRACT–ENGAGE–DELIVER (H1), and you are ready to
think about the form in which each of those phases should
take place. You may already be considering a setup that
sketches the interaction of a single person with your system.

◇◇◇

**Museums, exhibition centres and similar public places
are usually visited by groups of people. However, most
interactive systems can only be used by a single person at
a time.**

Standard user interface design mostly cares about the scenario in which one person interacts with a computer. The
term "Human–Computer Interaction" reflects this attitude,
which for many interactive systems is quite acceptable.
However, even when the social context of the user and his
task are taken into account, it is not normally considered

that the actual interaction can take place between two people sharing the same system. Those scenarios are rather dealt with in the discipline of computer-supported cooperative work (CSCW).

WorldBeat: 2 batons

The *WorldBeat* exhibit features not one, but two infrared batons to create musical input in many of its components. For example, the "Instant Salsa" setup, a part of the *Joy-Sticks* component, lets one user play a rhythmic Salsa pattern by swinging her baton up and down, while the second user can insert trumpet riffs and drum soli into the music by hitting downwards, or pressing the button on his baton. As the opening picture shows, users are having a lot of fun using the system in this way: instead of one user disappearing in a virtual world of interaction with a computer system, where only he knows what is happening, the system fades into the background and becomes a medium for two people to interact *with each other*, in this case musically. Its big advantage over normal human–human cooperation is that it can still augment the cooperation with subtle help, such as matching the notes created by both players onto a common musical scale.

Of course, there are many situations where especially control input cannot reasonably be shared between people. *WorldBeat*, for example, only lets one of its two batons control the on-screen pointer used for menu selection and other control input, and only one baton is active in the conducting component (two people conducting at the same time would not make much sense).

Bystanders

In addition to this active cooperative use, interactive exhibits should allow additional people to watch what is going on. This not only increases the number of visitors who can, at least in some way, experience the exhibit at the same time, it also helps them to prepare themselves if they are next in line to actively use it. This reduces subsequent learning time in the active usage phase, which also increases active visitor throughput. Moreover, it can attract passers-by who would never stop if all they saw is, say, a person staring into (and occluding) a small monitor.

The *CAVE* installation in the Ars Electronica Center in Linz, Austria, offers a high level of this type of cooperative experience: not only the main user, but a dozen additional people, all wearing special digital glasses, can enter a room where walls and floor are large displays creating the illusion of a three-dimensional reality. While only the main user has a control for moving around this virtual environment, and only his position affords an ideal three-dimensional view, all other users in the room can participate in this experience to a high degree. Other exhibits in this centre, such as a flight simulator, feature large monitors mirroring what the active user currently sees, thereby communicating his experience to bystanders.

The CAVE

Figure 4.19: Main user and bystanders in the AEC *CAVE*.

If cooperative experience is not planned, it will occur nevertheless. For example, where exhibits are equipped with headphones, people can often be observed sharing the single headphone set between them, awkwardly huddling together (and bending the headphone dangerously). What they are trying to do is to create a cooperative experience where the designer did not care to plan for one.

Unplanned cooperation

Therefore:

Allow two people to actively use your interactive exhibit together at the same time. Ensure that at least five bystanders can watch, listen to, or otherwise passively experience the exhibit while it is being used by somebody else.

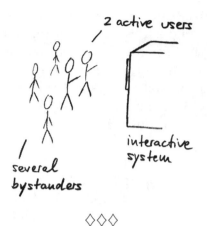

◇◇◇

Cooperative use often involves one user handing control over to the next—EASY HANDOVER (H4). Display size has to be chosen correctly to create the right level of immersion—IMMERSIVE DISPLAY (H13). . . .

H4   EASY HANDOVER *

Figure 4.20: A visitor waiting for her turn to use *WorldBeat*.

...you have found a way to attract users if the system is not presently in use—ATTRACTION SPACE (H2), and how to engage them and convey the system's messages to them—CLOSED LOOP (H9). Now you have to think about the situation when a user wants to "take over" from the previous visitor, a common situation in busy environments.

◇◇◇

Most interactive systems implicitly assume that each user begins using their system from a start page or initial state. At interactive exhibits, however, one user often takes over from the previous one, possibly in the middle of the interaction, and without knowing the interaction history of the previous user.

Most traditional, desktop-oriented interactive systems can be designed from a point of view where a user initiates the interaction from a defined starting point (for example by launching an application). Moreover, a typical user accesses such a system many times, and already knows something about the system when he accesses it.

User change in middle of interaction

At interactive exhibits, on the other hand, one user often leaves the "controls" to the next user without returning the system to its "idle" or initial state of interaction. This may happen because the first user wants the second user to "try out what I am just doing" (especially if he knows the other one), or he feels social pressure to leave the system for others who are waiting for their turn.

In the *WorldBeat* system, for example, visitors often take the batons from their predecessor while that user is in the middle of interacting with one of the system features. The two possible actions then (which have both been observed) are either that the new user continues to use the same feature (e.g., conducting), or that he uses the "back" button and chooses a different feature.

WorldBeat: No user-specific state

WorldBeat supports the first alternative by a design that has no user-specific state. The only state that users can create in a system is the position within the hierarchy of features (e.g., the fact that "conducting" is the currently active feature) and the settings of the controls within this feature (e.g., the solo instrument selected in the improvisation module). No personal data, such as names or digital photos of the user, is created in the system, so the user who takes over has no need to "reset" those values to his own settings.

Back button

The second alternative is supported by a "back" button that is available on every page of the system, and that always leads back up the hierarchical menu tree of available features.

In both cases, the new user cannot be expected to have seen the introductory screen explaining how the batons are used. This knowledge, however, is something that the new user has already gathered from watching his predecessor using the exhibit before taking over.

The *Virtual Vienna* exhibit, which lets users take a virtual tour of the city of Vienna, uses an even more stateless approach. The only parameters that users change by interacting with the exhibit are the current geographical position within the virtual environment, and the choice of language for the interface. It is not necessary to return to a specific "starting" point in the application to begin using the system, and the language can be changed at any time through a button that is always available.

Virtual Vienna

The HCI pattern collection by Tidwell [1998] contains a pattern BACK TO A SAFE PLACE, which represents a similar idea. It recommends to always supply users with a simple means of getting back to an initial, known, or otherwise "secure" state if they get lost in the course of interaction.

BACK TO A SAFE PLACE

Therefore:

Minimize the dialogue history that a new user needs to know to begin using an interactive exhibit. Offer a simple means to return the system to its initial state. If critical, user-specific parameters such as language need to be set by a user, let users change the setting at any time, no matter where they are in the system.

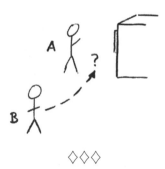

◇◇◇

If your system needs to present a multitude of information units (such as screen pages), arrange them so a new user can quickly find his way back to the main selection—FLAT AND NARROW TREE (H7). Minimize using information forms that depend on language or culture, at least for the basic information necessary to operate the exhibit and set the language—LANGUAGE INDEPENDENCE (H10). ...

H5   SIMPLE IMPRESSION *

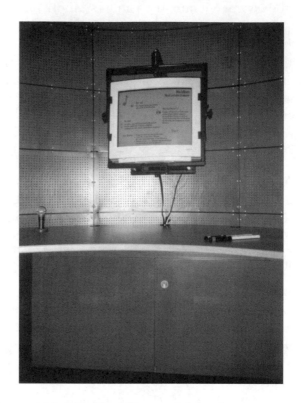

Figure 4.21: The *WorldBeat* exhibit when not in use.

. . . you have decided to create an attractive, innovative system—ATTRACTION SPACE (H2). Now you need to find a way to lure people into using your system, and not become frustrated with it.

◇◇◇

Interactive exhibits are supposed to convey often complex messages, and show the power and fascination of intricate new technology. However, users of such systems are typically first-time, and one-time users with no time to go through a long learning curve.

WorldBeat: Few, simple devices

The *WorldBeat* includes a complex variety of innovative hard- and software, such as infrared batons, or algorithms to retrieve songs through hummed queries. Its goal is to convey how computers support new ways to interact with music, so the power of those technologies is part of its message. However, the typical user has never before encountered the system, probably never will again, and only intends to spend a few minutes with it to "see what you can do here". Therefore, the system was designed to convey a very simple, inviting system image to the user. It only offers few, non-professional input devices (neither computer keyboard nor piano keyboard), no shortcuts to circumvent the hierarchical navigational structure, and often just one choice where more would have been simple to implement.

Some operating systems offer a specific "simple mode" of operation geared towards unexperienced users. It removes access to advanced features from the user interface, simplifying the impression that the system conveys. An example is the *Simple Finder* option in Mac OS®.

Simple Finder

Therefore:

Make the user interface of your interactive exhibit as simple as possible, and communicate this simplicity visually through the appearance of the system as a whole. Compromise usage efficiency, customizability, and feature-richness in favour of a system that is easy to use, no matter how advanced the underlying technology may be.

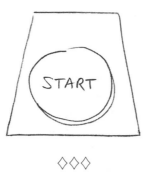

◇◇◇

To convey a simple impression, try hiding complex hardware from view—INVISIBLE HARDWARE (H14). To combine this initial impression with a rich set of available features, introduce them gradually upon user initiative—INCREMENTAL REVEALING (H6). . . .

H6   INCREMENTAL REVEALING **

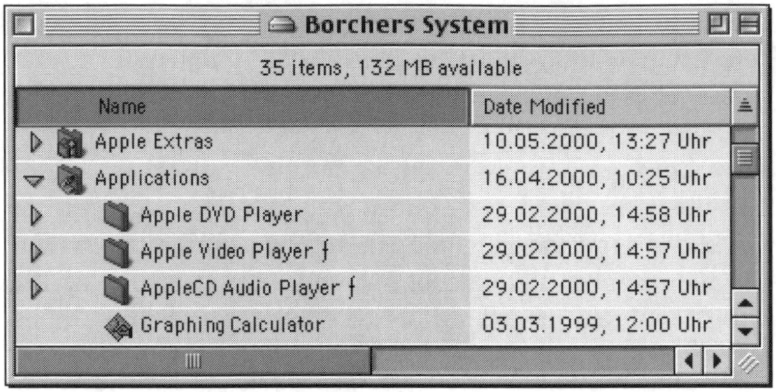

Figure 4.22: Lists of files in the Mac OS® Finder.

...you have sketched a design of your interface that conveys a simple impression—SIMPLE IMPRESSION (H5), yet your system has more complex features that you wish to offer in order to deliver its message—ATTRACT–ENGAGE–DELIVER (H1). Now you need to balance these two goals of simplicity and complexity.

◇◇◇

Systems that look complex from the start do not invite users. However, if a system does not offer enough complexity in its interaction possibilities, using it can quickly become boring.

WorldBeat: Main screen plus components

WorldBeat (see appendix B) is structured into a short introductory screen, followed by a simple main selection screen with only names and icons of the main exhibit components (conducting, improvising, etc.) No lengthy texts overwhelm the user. But at this point, he has only scratched the surface of the exhibit. The overall wealth of features is presented in a gradual way: if the user moves the pointer towards one of the component icons, a short explanation appears (first revealing stage). Then, if he selects it, a separate page opens up that explains the component in more detail (second revealing stage), and lets the user try it out.

Expanding list views

Most desktop operating systems, such as the Mac OS®

shown in the opening picture, offer views onto the file and folder hierarchy that initially only show top-level items. Only when the user is interested in the contents of one of those objects does it unfold to reveal the next level of detail of the file hierarchy in this part.

Therefore:

Initially, present only a very concise and simple overview of the system functionality. Only when users become active—showing that they are interested in a certain part of this overview—offer additional information about it, and gradually reveal what is lying "behind" this introductory presentation.

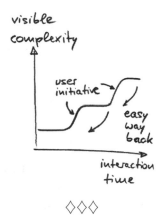

◇◇◇

Especially for information-oriented systems, a simple hierarchic structure to organize the revealing process is often useful—FLAT AND NARROW TREE (H7). To insert an additional revealing layer, and make the process more continuous, use temporary descriptions showing what the next revealing stage contains—DYNAMIC DESCRIPTOR (H15). . . .

H7   FLAT AND NARROW TREE *

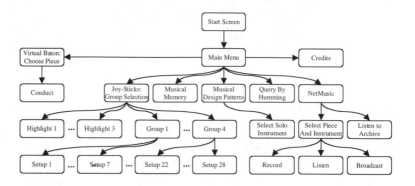

Figure 4.23: *WorldBeat* internal menu tree.

...you have decided about the overall structure of the interaction, and found a way to unfold the initially simple appearance of your system into its full complexity over the course of the interaction—INCREMENTAL REVEALING (H6). Now you should think about the total size of this unfolding structure.

◇◇◇

Many interactive exhibits consist of a number of "pages" through which the visitor can navigate. However, large information hierarchies, especially unordered networks with arbitrary links, quickly lead to disorientation.

WorldBeat menu tree

WorldBeat, whose menu tree is shown in the opening picture, consists of a start page that explains briefly what the exhibit is about, and how to use the batons, and then leads to a main selection screen where the user can choose one of the six *WorldBeat* components, go back to the start page, or read the credits for the system. The component pages in turn offer one or more choices to continue further into the respective component, or return to the main selection screen.

Interactive Fugue menu

The *Interactive Fugue* exhibit has a similar overall structure. The initial selection page leads to four subpages for its various features, which in turn lead the user through a sequence of subsequent pages to use those features.

The hierarchical organizing principle is ubiquitous in electronic systems and user interfaces. It is at the heart of the directory structure of the file system of all major operating systems, and replicated in their graphical "folder" view of the file system. It is also a general user interface pattern described by Tidwell [1998] as HIERARCHICAL SET.

If the hierarchy is kept small enough, the current position can be remembered well, and the navigation metaphor be used confidently, even by computer novices. A commonly quoted maximum capacity of human short-term memory and processing is around seven chunks of information [Miller, 1956], so this is both a good estimate for an upper limit on the number of entries from which the user can choose at each level. The maximum path length should be even shorter to avoid people forgetting where in the tree structure they are.

Seven information chunks

Therefore:

Use a tree-like hierarchy to organize the content of your exhibit. Make the tree no more than 5 levels deep, and put no more than 7 branches into any node.

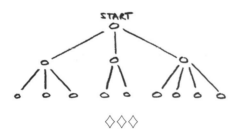

◇◇◇

Not all exhibits need to have this hierarchical layout. Systems that aim to convey one specific computer-supported experience can use realistic navigation styles— AUGMENTED REALITY (H8). . . .

H8   AUGMENTED REALITY *

Figure 4.24: The *DynaWall* environment [Streitz et al., 1999].

. . . you are designing an interactive exhibit, and have to decide whether to structure your contents into a logical information hierarchy—FLAT AND NARROW TREE (H7), or use an approach that creates an immersive experience in which the information structure is not the primary dimension.

◇◇◇

On the one hand, interactive exhibits generally aim to convey an innovative experience. On the other hand, they have to relate to the corpus of real experiences users already have, to be easy to understand.

DynaWall

The *DynaWall* project shown in the opening picture [Streitz et al., 1999] uses a series of interactive whiteboards to create a large touch-sensitive "electronic wall" where users can work with large information structures collaboratively. It does not require anybody to enter a virtual environment. Instead, it resembles a standard chalk board arrangement, but augments this infrastructure with the advantages and added possibilities of an interactive computer display.

Virtual Vienna city tour

The *Virtual Vienna* city tour uses the metaphor of a real city tour to become easier to understand for visitors at first sight. Users do not browse an artificial information space like a web document network, or put on a VR helmet which would only add to preparation time, and reduce visitor throughput and possible cooperation. Instead, they start out as on a real city tour, beginning with a panoramic view on a large projection before them, of one of the important places in the city. This spatial city tour metaphor always remains the main metaphor for using the system. Information about objects of interest in the current place is displayed by moving towards those objects, which brings up a short explanation about them. To move to a different panorama, users can follow direction arrows displayed within the 3-D view.

Users navigate by moving a *NaviPad*, a console comparable to a flight stick, but with two handles, with their hands to turn around, look up and down, and move towards or away from objects in the scene. As in a real tour, practically their entire viewing field is filled with this photorealistic panorama. Only if they wish to get an overview of the city's geography, and a sense where they are in the city, they can have a look at an LCD panel between their hands with a map. This situation is very similar to walking through a city with a real map in your hands. Of course, the interactive technology makes the digital map more useful in some respects. For example, to move to a distant part of the city, users do not have to walk through all the panoramas on the way, but can jump directly to the point of interest by touching it on the map.

NaviPad

The entire research direction of *ubiquitous and pervasive computing* aims at a similar experience: users are not taken into a virtual reality in which real experiences can only be recreated inadequately. Instead, their real environment is augmented by unobtrusive, ubiquitous, intelligent technology, systems and applications that, for example, add active markers to books, remind the user of errands when he passes a shop, etc. [Russell and Weiser, 1998].

Ubiquitous and
Pervasive Computing

Therefore:

In situations where your system aims to recreate a real experience, use as much real instead of virtual environ-

ment as possible. Instead of trying to recreate all aspects of reality inside an artificial environment, augment the real environment with interactive technology that is not usually available otherwise.

◇◇◇

Augmented reality works the better, the less obtrusive and visible the actual technology is—INVISIBLE HARDWARE (H14). . . .

H9 CLOSED LOOP *

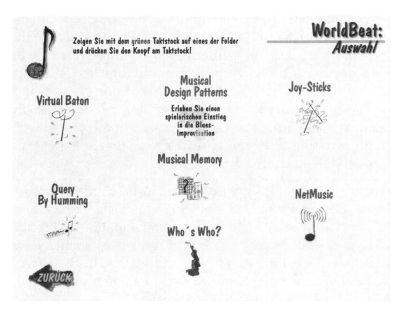

Figure 4.25: *WorldBeat* main selection screen.

... you are designing an interactive exhibit or similar public system, and a very general structure of interacting with your system is in place—ATTRACT–ENGAGE–DELIVER (H1). Now you need to find a way to wrap possibly many different features of your system into understandable units for the user.

◇◇◇

A public interactive system may have many features to explore and messages to convey. However, casual users will not engage with a system for a long time if they do not feel they are getting something out of it.

The *WorldBeat* exhibit includes features to find tunes by humming, improvise to a band, play virtual instruments, guess instrument sounds, and others, many of them with several subsections to explore and try out. It would take about an hour to work through all of its functions; this is far more time than the average user wants (and is expected)

WorldBeat: Closed experience per feature

to spend with the system. To make sure that every visitor still experiences a gratifying interaction, those features are offered as alternative choices from a central selection page, which is always just two clicks away from anywhere in the exhibit structure. Upon entering one of those features, its message is explained very briefly, and after trying it out, the user is lead back to the central selection page, which he usually already knows. At this point, a user can easily leave the system, or pass on to the next waiting visitor, with a feeling of closedness because he knows that he has at least explored that feature now.

Eight Golden Rules

The same principle applies to standard computer applications: Shneiderman [1998, p. 75], in his *Eight Golden Rules* of interface design, includes a recommendation to "design dialogs to yield closure": Action sequences should have an obvious beginning, middle, and end, with clear feedback about the completion of such a sequence to convey the sense of accomplishment to the user.

Therefore:

After two to four minutes of interaction, explain to the user what she has just seen or learned from your system, guide her back to a central starting point in it that she recognizes, and offer the opportunity to leave the system, or to continue exploring another aspect of it.

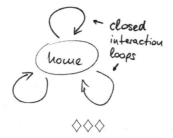

◇◇◇

A good way to make sure the interaction loops are easy to recognize is to arrange contents in a clear hierarchy—FLAT AND NARROW TREE (H7). To guide people along those loops, you should always just bother them with the information necessary at each point—INFORMATION JUST IN TIME (H16). ...

H10 LANGUAGE INDEPENDENCE

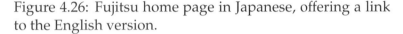

Figure 4.26: Fujitsu home page in Japanese, offering a link to the English version.

... you have mapped out most of your interaction design, and your system allows users to begin interacting with it even when it is not in its initial state—EASY HANDOVER (H4). But as you think about filling the system design with contents, the question of language invariably comes up.

◇◇◇

Initially, most applications are designed with only one language for the user interface in mind. Exhibits in public spaces, however, often have international visitors who may not speak the local language.

Most interactive exhibits have to convey part of their message in textual (written or spoken) form, and therefore need to decide on a set of natural languages to support. It is not sufficient, however, to just allow language selection on the start page of an exhibit, without any further support, since new users may take over the exhibit when it is in some other interaction state. At least the way to language settings itself has to be clearly recognizable from any point within the system.

As an example, in the *Virtual Vienna* exhibit, a link to the language selection is always available in a corner of the display showing the map of the city tour.

Virtual Vienna:
Language selector

The same is true for web pages; the Japanese Fujitsu web site shown above always shows an English language selection button—an essential piece of help for users looking for information in English.

Flags

Flags are a commonly observed way to represent language choices. As Pemberton [1998] points out, however, it may not be suitable to represent a language by a single flag. Many languages are the official language in several countries, many countries have several different spoken languages, and some even have more than one official language. Flag groups are sometimes used to solve the problem in a politically more correct way, but consider that there are about 200 flag symbols versus 4–5000 different spoken languages worldwide, so a flag suggests that you support all languages spoken in that country. A more natural solution is to put a list of all available language names, written in their own respective language, onto the interface object that leads to language selection.

Therefore:

No matter in what state your interactive exhibit is, always provide a pictorial or multilingual way to access language settings.

◇◇◇

This is a basic pattern that has no further references within this pattern language.

H11 DOMAIN-APPROPRIATE DEVICES *

Figure 4.27:   A visitor using the *WorldBeat* exhibit. For a video example of this system in use, see ⟨http://www.actibits.com/⟩.

... you have decided about the application area of your interactive system, and you are trying to make it attractive and cooperative—ATTRACTION SPACE (H2), COOPERATIVE EXPERIENCE (H3). Now, you have to decide how the user should physically interact with your system.

◇◇◇

Interactive systems are used in a huge variety of application domains. Yet, they almost invariably use standard input and output devices.

Every interactive software system has a domain in which it is used, or which it addresses, and that its contents or functions are about. The application domain of a computer-based drawing course, for example, is the artistic domain of drawing, and the application domain of a power plant process control system is that power plant with its functions.

However, most interactive systems have been using the

Many metaphors, few devices

standard keyboard and mouse as input devices, plus a monitor as output device, but nothing else. User interface designers put a lot of work into creating "metaphors" in which the virtual, on-screen world resembles items and concepts from the well-known, physical world. But all the while, those objects remain virtual, volatile images on a standard screen to be manipulated with the same, generic set of input devices and physical actions: type, point, click.

A claim that is often heard is that incorporating dedicated input and output devices is too expensive. But often, it is not even attempted to estimate the amount of extra work and its possible payoff, because it requires a lot of thinking from the designers to come up with new ideas apart from mouse and keyboard, and it is an area where products and standards are not as comfortably developed and accessible as in the world of standard input devices.

Figure 4.28: A domain-appropriate control to adjust a car seat [Norman, 1988].

Natural mappings

But psychological research as well as common sense tell us that users are much more efficient, successful, and satisfied when they are offered I/O devices that resemble physical objects of the application domain. For example, Norman [1988, pp. 23 ff.] talks in detail about the advantages of "natural mappings" from input device to system function, and gives a good example of a device perfectly designed for its dedicated purpose: a car seat adjustment control that is shaped like a miniature seat itself. To adjust his own seat, the user simply pushes the corresponding part of the miniature seat into the desired direction. It would have been far more cumbersome to understand and use the seat controls if they had been designed as a set of industry-standard buttons on the dashboard (and, if we imagine using those controls ourselves, it would probably also have been less fun).

The same is true for the *WorldBeat* system shown in the opening picture: it is an interactive exhibit that demonstrates to its users how computers open up new ways to interact with music, from conducting a computer orchestra, to improvising to a blues band with computer support. While our initial designs included a standard keyboard and mouse as input devices, we gradually found out that we did not really need them, and that they would spoil the "musical atmosphere" that the exhibit tries to create. The two infrared batons, on the other hand, are artefacts that resemble a conductor's baton, or xylophone sticks—objects that are well known from the musical domain. In taking them up, the user is already led away from thinking about interacting with a computer, into an experience of interacting with music. The system was elected one of the three most popular exhibits in the centre where it is installed [Borchers, 1997], and received an award for its new way to convey musical concepts.

WorldBeat: batons
for music

Figure 4.29: *Urp* simulates wind between two physical building models [MIT Media Lab, 2000 / Underkoffler and Ishii, 1999].

Ishii and Ullmer [1997] developed the concept of *Tangible Bits*, where the gap between human and computer is bridged by "coupling digital information to everyday

Urp: Tangible Bits

physical objects and environments". For example, they created an *Urban Planning Workbench (Urp)* where buildings are represented by physical models that can be moved around on a map of the neighbourhood. Effects such as shadows and airflow are simulated in response to the physical placement of the objects and projected onto the map. Informal studies showed that most architects who tried the system would use it immediately if available [Underkoffler and Ishii, 1999]. This is another example of the advantages of dedicated, application-specific devices.

Therefore:

From the plethora of available input and output devices, choose devices that resemble real objects from the application domain of your interactive system. Whenever users have to input something, or receive information from your system, determine whether the standard periphery is really the best choice for this purpose, or if other devices can make working with the system more intuitive, efficient, and enjoyable.

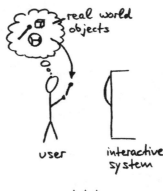

◇◇◇

A new device is also a good starting point to create a system that looks fresh, different, and intriguing— INNOVATIVE APPEARANCE (H12), and that does not look like "a computer"—INVISIBLE HARDWARE (H14). If your interactive system requires different forms of input, it may be feasible to map them to your new input device—ONE INPUT DEVICE (H17). ...

H12   INNOVATIVE APPEARANCE *

Figure 4.30: *Rhythm Tree* interactive music system [MIT Media Lab, 2000].

...you are designing an interactive exhibit, and you have decided to attract visitors in some way—ATTRACTION SPACE (H2). Now you need to find methods to establish this attraction.

◇◇◇

The most established user interface hardware and software is often also the most boring.

The *WorldBeat* music exhibit uses infrared batons as input devices. They are unlike anything visitors have normally used up to now to interact with a computer, which makes the exhibit look interesting and promises an experience from which something new can be learned.

WorldBeat: batons

The *Virtual Vienna* city tour uses a custom-designed

Virtual Vienna: NaviPad

NaviPad to move around in the three-dimensional photo-realistic panoramas. The same degrees of freedom could be made accessible through a standard joystick and additional slider, but they would not only be less appropriate for the domain of a city tour, but also less innovative for visitors than a custom-designed device. It is often enough to "wrap" standard devices into an innovative outer shape to decouple the impression of the system from known modes of interaction.

Brain Opera: Rhythm Tree

The *Brain Opera* music exhibit by the MIT Media Lab features, among other parts, large rubber forms resembling ears, noses, etc. that can be punched and pressed by visitors to create various sounds (see the opening picture). The shape and physical mode of operation of these input devices alone are intriguing enough to attract people to use this exhibit who would hardly have stopped to achieve the same results at a computer exibit solely equipped with mouse and keyboard.

Therefore:

Choose input and output devices that look different from standard computing periphery. Raise the curiosity of visitors by offering new channels and modalities of interaction as part of the user experience.

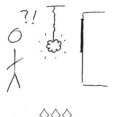

◇◇◇

If the subject of the exhibit does not happen to be technology itself, it is usually more attractive to hide standard hardware—INVISIBLE HARDWARE (H14). The new appearance of your system, with some new modality of interaction, may even allow you to do away with other more standard devices—ONE INPUT DEVICE (H17). . . .

H13 IMMERSIVE DISPLAY *

Figure 4.31: *CAVE* in the Ars Electronica Center Linz.

...you have decided to create an exhibit that several people can experience simultaneously—COOPERATIVE EXPERIENCE (H3). Now you need to find a way to design the visual output of such a system.

◇◇◇

Typical usage scenarios of standard computer systems often involve only one human interacting with the computer at any time, and the system is only a small part of the real environment of the user. But exhibits are usually visited by groups of people, and when users interact with them, they are ready to immerse themselves into the world of the exhibit.

The *CAVE* installation in the Ars Electronica Center in Linz uses wall-size projections all around the visitors to immerse them into a virtual reality. Special glasses synchronize with these displays to create a three-dimensional impression.

CAVE: 3-D walls

Virtual Vienna uses a rear-projected display screen of about

Virtual Vienna:
panorama

1.6 m width, with the users standing at the same distance to the screen. This fills most of the optical viewing field when looking at the screen, and helps people to feel like they are actually standing at the place whose panorama is being displayed.

Personal Orchestra:
large projection

Personal Orchestra uses an even bigger display area of about 2.5 m width, again with a corresponding viewing distance. This conveys the impression of actually standing in front of the Vienna Philharmonic in a far better way than it would on a small computer monitor.

With these systems, this large display not only immerses the main user into the experience, it also allows several bystanders to at least observe the exhibit in action, which many may find already sufficient without becoming an active user.

Therefore:

Prefer a single exhibit with a large-scale display, with a minimum of 1.5 m in display width, over several similar stations with smaller displays, and over other output devices that shield a single user from his co-visitors, such as head-mounted displays. Design for a viewing distance that roughly equals the width of the display.

◇◇◇

If you hide the display technology, it can become a "magic image"—INVISIBLE HARDWARE (H14). ...

H14 INVISIBLE HARDWARE *

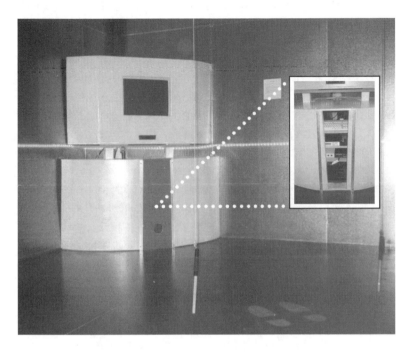

Figure 4.32: Hiding *WorldBeat* hardware.

... you have designed an attractive, interesting user interface—INNOVATIVE APPEARANCE (H12), DOMAIN-APPROPRIATE DEVICES (H11), IMMERSIVE DISPLAY (H13), and you now need to decide how to set up your exhibit, what users should see from your system, and what should be hidden, so that the system does not look too threateningly complex—SIMPLE IMPRESSION (H5).

◇◇◇

Modern exhibits often feature complicated and expensive hardware. The user, however, may be driven away by the display of such technology.

The opening picture shows the *WorldBeat* system in an exhibition in the *Techniek Museum Delft*. *WorldBeat* consists of many technical hardware components, including a computer, MIDI (Musical Instruments Digital Interface) connector, baton interface, pitch-to-MIDI converter, Hi-Fi ampli-

WorldBeat:
Hardware hidden in cabinet

fier, battery charger, various power adaptors, and some 30 m of cabling. It was tempting to show at least some of this technology to the user, to give an impression of the complexity of the system behind the scenes. However, the exhibit was supposed to be about *music*, and it would be hard enough not to scare off people because they expect to need expert musical skills to operate the exhibit. Showing all the technology to them would have, in addition, created the impression that one surely has to be a computer expert to use such a complex system. This would have created a contact threshold for users approaching the system. Therefore, our design went into the opposite extreme, and hid all hardware except what was necessary to run the user interface—infrared batons, infrared tracker and microphone as input, and monitor as output device. The result was that people without any prior computer knowledge used the exhibit confidently, and only after using it, would some more technically minded visitors enquire about the technology at work.

Film projectors

This principle has also been expressed by Norman [1988], and he gives a good example of its application. Old film projectors required the user to manually thread the film into the transport mechanism. The complexity of this task was only partially reduced by later threading support mechanisms that still left the task visible. Today's video recorder fulfils a similar task—threading the video tape around the video heads—, but this complex mechanism is hidden completely from the user, who triggers this process by just pushing a video cassette into the recorder.

Therefore:

Hide as much of the computer-related hardware of your interactive exhibit as possible. Only leave visible those devices that the user has to see, and that generate an image adequate for the application domain of your exhibit.

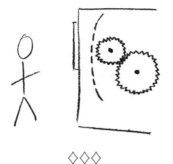

◇◇◇

You can reduce the apparent complexity of your system further by reducing the number of user interface devices — ONE INPUT DEVICE (H17). ...

H15 DYNAMIC DESCRIPTOR **

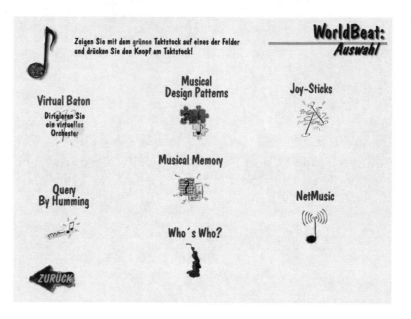

Figure 4.33: Dynamic descriptor help in *WorldBeat*.

... you have decided to organize your system into separate units of information or function that the user encounters gradually when exploring the system—INCREMENTAL REVEALING (H6). You may have organized your contents into a hierarchy—FLAT AND NARROW TREE (H7). Now you have to find a way to inform the user in advance about the upcoming features or information on subsequent "pages".

◇◇◇

Users need help on the virtual objects that they are interacting with. However, conveying all this information all the time would overcrowd the information space.

Mac OS®: Balloon
Help

The Mac OS® operating system uses icons with names to represent files, folders, disks, printers, and many other objects in its user interface. However, even experienced users occasionally need some basic information about an object, for example to find out what application created a certain file. Referring to printed documentation, or even to an online manual, would interrupt the task too much. Displaying all this information for every visible object all the time would clutter the screen. The solution introduced by Apple is called "Balloon Help", and it shows a short description in a bubble next to any item that the mouse pointer touches. This feature needs to be switched on explicitly, because it creates a certain visual disturbance, and the average user, who has already gained some experience with the system, does not even want to see this information appear dynamically everywhere she points.

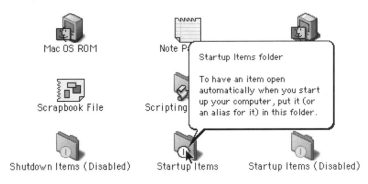

Figure 4.34: Mac OS® Balloon help, explaining an object under the pointer on-screen.

Microsoft Windows® features a similar mechanism called "ToolTips". The general pattern has been identified by Tidwell [1998] as SHORT DESCRIPTION, and the INTERACT patterns workshop [Borchers et al., 2001] used a similar pattern, DESCRIPTION AT YOUR FINGERTIPS, as stand-alone example of a typical HCI design pattern.

The situation in interactive exhibits is different, however: the typical user is a first-time, one-time user. He has no experience with the system, and will probably never encounter it again. Therefore, no long-term learning curve development can be assumed, and such dynamic descriptions need to be provided automatically by the system, without requiring explicit user action.

In the *WorldBeat* exhibit, for example, when a user moves

WorldBeat: dynamic feature explanation

the baton cursor over a selectable item on the main selection screen, the icon fades into the background, and a short explanatory text of lains what the component is about that can be reached via this item (see the opening image). This design allows users to explore what awaits them inside the various components, deciding on what they would like to try first or next, without having to enter all the components to find out what they are about. It adds another, intermediate layer of detail between the opening page and the subsequent component pages.

Voice mailbox

Other media types can use a similar concept. Voice mailbox systems usually let the user quickly progress through their menus, with short announcements that can be stopped at any time, but when the user remains idle for a while, additional context-sensitive information on the current menu, its options, and use, is frequently played back.

With all these examples, it is crucial that the description be rendered in close spatial or temporal vicinity of the original object, as it may otherwise be overlooked. For example, Zellweger et al. [2000] show that textual descriptions take users longer to read, and are more frequently overlooked, if they are placed away from the on-screen text that triggers their appearance.

Therefore:

Provide one sentence of information on any user interface objects that are not self-explanatory. Activate this information automatically, dynamically, and close to such an object whenever the user has focused attention on it.

◇◇◇

This is a basic pattern that has no further references within this pattern language.

H16 INFORMATION JUST IN TIME **

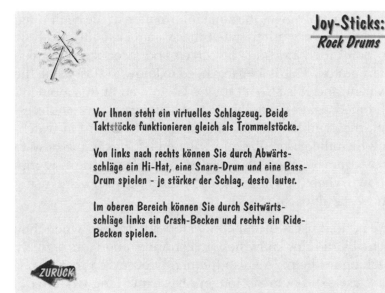

Figure 4.35: *WorldBeat* screen for the *Rock Drums* feature.

... you are deciding when to explain features to the user—
INCREMENTAL REVEALING (H6), and when to convey your
messages so people remain in control of where they are and
what they have learned—CLOSED LOOP (H9).

◇◇◇

**Occasionally, a system needs to explain how to continue,
but exhibit users do not read long instructions, let alone
memorize them.**

Not to strain short-term memory with complex instructions   Spare short-term
to be remembered is one of the most established user in-   memory
terface guidelines (see, e.g., [Shneiderman, 1998, p. 75]).
Graphical user interfaces address this issue with the concept of "see and choose instead of remember and type in"
[Shneiderman, 1998, p. 236]. However, with interactive exhibits, the situation is again more drastic. They often need
to explain an unusual form of interaction, but at the same
time there is a lack of long learning time or frequent use.

Moreover, users may not even have seen instructions on a previous screen—EASY HANDOVER (H4).

WorldBeat only gives minimal information at the beginning, explaining very briefly what the system is about, and how to point the batons at the screen and select an on-screen start button. This is all users need to know to start using the system, and it is also all they wish to read at this moment. If someone takes over the system being used by a predecessor, they will have collected this information from watching the other user. Each instruction—for example how to play drums using the batons (see opening picture)—is only shown when the system is ready to let the user begin using the respective feature.

WorldBeat:
Condensed
explanations

We noticed users usually only stopping to read when they actually did not know how to continue, and were actively looking for help. We also frequently observed that *World-Beat* users did not read longer texts explaining what to do, until those texts were redesigned to be even more succinct, clear, and constructive, as shown in the opening picture.

Therefore:

Delay usage instructions until users actually need to know about them to continue, and keep them as short as possible, usually no more than three sentences with twelve words each.

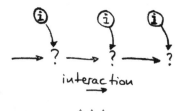

◇◇◇

If space is limited, you can make this information appear dynamically only when needed—DYNAMIC DESCRIPTON (H15). . . .

H17   ONE INPUT DEVICE *

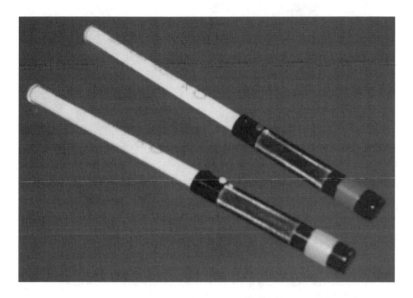

Figure 4.36: *Lightning II* infrared batons (by Buchla and Associates) used in the *WorldBeat* exhibit.

... you have found a way to create an interface adequate for the domain of your system—DOMAIN-APPROPRIATE DEVICES (H11) that looks interesting to use—INNOVATIVE APPEARANCE (H12). Now is the time to see whether the various input channels can be simplified, so that the number of devices that the user needs to see may be reduced—INVISIBLE HARDWARE (H14).

◇◇◇

Many interactive systems require a variety of different input devices to be used. Some systems may be able to recognize gestures without any physical input device to touch. But interactive exhibits are used by people with no prior experience with the system who are confused by a large number of input devices, and feel uneasy with no device at all.

The initial interface design sketches for the *WorldBeat* system included the following devices:

WorldBeat: From many to few devices

- two infrared batons,

- a microphone,

- a mouse,

- a computer keyboard,

- a piano keyboard,

- a video camera,

- a data glove.

The list partially reflected our desire to integrate advanced features into the system. An example is the piano keyboard, which we originally planned as an alternative interface for professional musicians. We later removed those devices to achieve simplicity and arrive at a system understandable for the average short-time visitor. However, the list also contained devices that we simply assumed as necessary for a computer-based exhibit, such as mouse and computer keyboard, for example to let visitors select items on screen or enter their names. Such functions were later mapped to the batons (such as item selection), or turned out not to be necessary for the exhibit (such as typing in information).

The final user interface was reduced to just include batons, microphone, and monitor. Computer keyboard and mouse are hidden in a cabinet for maintenance, and a professional piano keyboard is stored elsewhere, but can be connected for special events or occasions.

Interactive Fugue:
From text to photo

In the *Interactive Fugue* system, we used a similar approach, and replaced the feature to enter names by a digital photo of the user that is automatically taken.

Zero input devices?

With *WorldBeat*, it would have been possible to go even further, and use gesture recognition instead of a physical input device. Just waving their arms around, however, makes many people feel insecure and silly; it turns out that most users like having something in their hands that shows their purpose when interacting.

Using just one instead of several devices, if sufficient for the task, is in accordance with standard usability heuristics, such as the principle of *Simple and Natural Dialogue:* "User interfaces should be simplified as much as possible, since every additional feature or item of information on a screen is one more thing to learn, one more thing to possibly misunderstand, and one more thing to search through when looking for the thing you want." [Nielsen, 1993, p. 115].

Therefore:

Give the user one input device to use your interactive exhibit—no less, and no more if possible. Simplify your interaction requirements until all interaction easily maps to this device.

◇◇◇

Make sure that the device you decide to leave in your system is still reminiscent of the application area—DOMAIN-APPROPRIATE DEVICES (H11). . . .

This concludes the pattern languages for HCI design issues that are specific to interactive music exhibits and other public systems. The next section deals with patterns that are used in the design and implementation of such systems.

4.3   Software Pattern Language

As Gamma et al. [1995] suggested, domain-specific software design patterns are important to supplement the general ones. There are many general software design patterns that could be identified in the systems designed by the author, but this section will concentrate on those patterns that relate specifically to software design for interactive music systems (see Fig. 4.37, as well as [Borchers and Mühlhäuser, 1998]).

No UML

These patterns follow the requirements outlined in the last chapter, and consequently do not use notations such as UML that may allow for more exact specification of solution details but are unknown to people from outside the software engineering profession. Instead, diagrams show relations between objects with clear-text explanations.

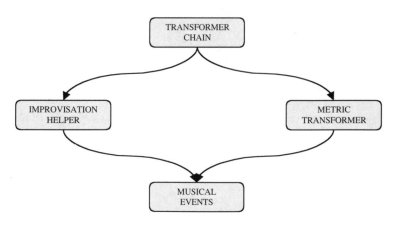

Figure 4.37: Software design patterns for interactive music systems identified in the various projects.

S1 BRANCHING TRANSFORMER CHAIN

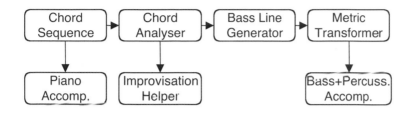

Figure 4.38: Chain of transformers in *WorldBeat*.

...you are building an interactive music system, and are now thinking about the overall architecture of its various signal-processing modules.

◇◇◇

If a software system is to react interactively to incoming musical data, it has to perform various processing steps on this data. However, the way in which these processing steps are to be combined is not always obvious.

The *Musical Design Patterns* component in the *WorldBeat exhibit* (see chapter 5) features the following overall structure to manipulate the accompaniment musical data stream, as shown in the opening diagram:

WorldBeat: Musical Design Patterns

1. The data source is a file containing a sequence of note chords for the accompaniment. These chords are also branched off directly to create the piano accompaniment. However, the system architecture does not rely on the complete data being available a priori, so it would be equally possible to use data arriving in real time, for example from a human accompanist.

2. The next transformer applied to this data stream is the root-finding *Chord Analyser,* which turns the data into an information stream containing the "root key" and mode of the current chord. This simple and coarse data is then branched off to the *Improvisation Helper,* which adjusts the scale of note pitches available for improvisation to ensure harmonic coherence.

3. Next, this stream is used by the *Bass Line Generator* to create a more detailed sequence of quarter notes that make an appropriate accompanying bass line for this chord.

4. The *Metric Transformer* then takes the resulting note sequence, creates a matching percussion accompaniment, and then slightly transforms the data by shifting some of the notes in percussion as well as bass line back in time to create a swinging feeling in the music.

5. The resulting musical stream of notes for percussion and bass line is played back to add to the piano accompaniment.

Personal Orchestra:
Conducting

A similar structure is found in the *Personal Orchestra* system, where users conduct a video and audio recording of an orchestra:

1. The incoming data stream, in this case in real time, represents the current position of the user's baton in x and y coordinates.

2. The first transformer applied to this stream detects downward beat gestures as turning points, and branches those events off to a counter object that keeps track of the rather crude measure of how many beats the user has conducted.

3. A subsequent processor analyses the data stream more closely, and determines how large the gestures currently are, and where they point. This data is then branched off to the sound mixing subsystem to determine overall volume and channel mixing balances of the audio track that is being played back.

4. Finally, a very detailed analysis compares the current baton position with the current position in playback, and from the exact difference computes parameters to

adjust the playback speed in order to follow the conductor's movements as closely as possible, and gradually synchronize the "clocks" of the conductor and the playback.

Therefore:

Use a chain of software objects that process the incoming musical data in sequence. Order the transformations so that coarse rhythmic, harmonic and melodic changes are applied before finer-grained adjustments.

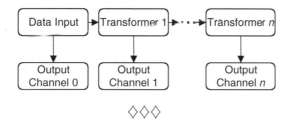

$$\diamond\diamond\diamond$$

Due to their time-based nature, rhythmic adjustments in such a chain require special consideration—METRIC TRANSFORMER (S2). The chain can also be routed through a component that uses this information to adjust another incoming signal which is created spontaneously—IMPROVISATION HELPER (S3). ...

S2   METRIC TRANSFORMER *

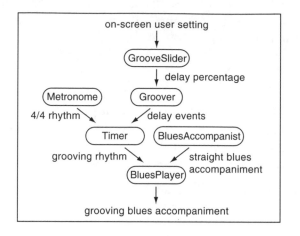

Figure 4.39: Groove transformer module in *WorldBeat*.

. . . you are designing a software system that needs to manipulate incoming musical data in real time. You have found an overall system architecture that allows you to process the incoming signal via a series of transformation procedures—BRANCHING TRANSFORMER CHAIN (S1). Now, you need to think about how to implement the transformation of rhythmical information.

◇◇◇

Musical performance adds countless subtle variations to the lifeless representation of a piece in a musical score or simple MIDI file. While these variations concern all musical dimensions—harmony, melody, and rhythm—, the one-dimensionality of time makes rhythm the most accessible concept for computer modelling. However, the time dependence of rhythm information also complicates the processing, especially if the system cannot rely on having all data available before the transformation begins.

The goal of this pattern is to show how to model timing deviations—small temporal changes within a beat from a fixed, uniform tempo as put down in a score, which make musical performance more human and vivid. Examples of such changes are (i) the *groove* in jazz music (see below),

(ii) the statistical deviations from the exact beat timing typical of natural performance, and (iii) the capability of a real band to follow a human rhythm even though it is not uniformly spaced.

The so-called *groove* in jazz is a good example of this concept: it is an often triolic shift of the intermediate beat in the rhythm section of a band to make the music "swing". It is explained in more detail in the musical design pattern TRIPLET GROOVE (M9).

The *WorldBeat* exhibit models this concept in software, and makes it accessible to the user. A *Creator* object uses pre-recorded musical material or quantized (i.e., metrically straightened) input from a performer to add groove to. A *Modulator* then models the groove with a simple delay algorithm. The delay is defined as the percentage of the time between two beats at which the intermediate beat is placed. 50% equal a straight, march-like style, 67% result in a triolic swing. Timings behind that create an even more "laid-back" style used in slow blues, while timings before 50% give an unusual, driving feeling in the music. An on-screen slider serves as *Customizer* to let the user choose this percentage while the music is playing, so that he can hear the result immediately. This has proven to be didactically very valuable. Current electronic instruments like keyboards, on the other hand, do not have anything similar to offer.

WorldBeat: Triplet Groove

Most commercial digital audio software products, for example *Studio Vision Pro* by Opcode, Inc., include another feature that can be implemented using this concept: they offer the ability to add *jitter*, i.e., the slight unsteadiness in timing inherent to natural musical performance, to a recorded (MIDI) piece. Computer-generated rhythms otherwise sound very artifical and lifeless. In this case, a *Modulator* can create this jitter using a statistical standard distribution of time deviations from the standard beat, although more sophisticated models are of course possible. A *Customizer* offers the user one or more sliders to change the distribution parameters interactively. In this case, some notes would be moved to an earlier point, so simultaneous real

Jitter in human recordings

time input (from a *Metronome*) and output (by a *Player* to a *Realizer*) are not possible.

WorldBeat: Virtual Baton

Finally, *WorldBeat* contains a *Virtual Baton* component where users can control tempo and dynamics of a piece by conducting with an infrared baton. In this conducting feature, the system does not use its internal timing, but follows the *human rhythm* of a conductor or band leader. In this case, the *Modulator* is implemented as a component that detects the beats in the human input. The *Metronome* just defines the basic tempo at the beginning, and the *Customizer* can offer settings to the user, such as the speed with which the computer adjusts to a sudden change of tempo by the conductor, from "immediately" (possibly dropping notes in case of a tempo increase) to "gradually" (spreading out the change over an adjustable time interval).

Personal Orchestra: Adjustable orchestra responsiveness

Personal Orchestra offers a similar scenario. Here, the above function of the *Customizer* is actually implemented as a parameter that the museum staff can adjust for different scenarios. The average user gets along better with an orchestra that reacts more slowly, ignoring short inadvertent tempo fluctuations, whereas a professional conductor can be offered a tighter coupling where the orchestra immediately reacts to subtle variations in the conducting input.

Some of the objects identified in the examples have architectural features that have also been described as general patterns in the literature. For example, introducing the dedicated *Modulator* object shields the other objects from changes in the method used to vary the timing. This concept is known as the STRATEGY software design pattern [Gamma et al., 1995].

Therefore:

To apply rhythmic transformations to an incoming musical data stream, create a subsystem consisting of the following six collaborating objects:

- **The *Creator* supplies the musical "raw material", i.e., the score to be played.**

- The *Metronome* supplies the "raw rhythm", i.e., the uniform beat at the general tempo of the piece.

- The *Modulator* defines the variation of any basic rhythm, in terms of the deviations to make from that rhythmic "spacing". The modulation can be based on fixed, random, or human deviations. This is where the semantic concept of metric transformation is modelled. In cases where gradual tempo changes also affect the future tempo as a whole, the *Modulator* can feed these changes back to the *Metronome*.

- The *Customizer* lets the user change parameters of the *Modulator* in real time. It defines the interaction metaphor when varying the metric transformation.

- The *Timer* takes the basic beat from the *Metronome*, and modifies it according to the input from the *Modulator*. Its output is the modulated beat that this pattern is supposed to model.

- The *Player* takes the musical material from the *Creator*, and the modulated beat from the *Timer*, and outputs the material in this rhythmic form, still in the shape of musical symbolic events (comparable to notes).

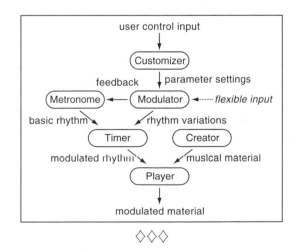

◇◇◇

Moving events back
in time

If the *Modulator* is built to move some notes back in time (i.e., to an earlier point than the t_0 scheduled by the *Metronome*) by up to $\delta t_{\max}$, then the time of the next beat and the material to play there have to be known in advance, at the latest at time $t_0 - \delta t_{\max}$. Thus, if the musical input arrives live from a human performer, then the system will not be able to apply this pattern and still deliver its part simultaneously to the input.

Advantages

From the semantic modelling perspective, the *MetricTransformer* pattern offers an approach to capture various types of human factors in rhythmical performance in a single framework. It can represent "knowledge" about how to enrich the concept of rhythm in a musical system, using mathematical definitions as well as external, human input to describe subtle deviations from a uniform beat.

For software engineering, the pattern shows how to design an interactive music system that deals with this richer concept of rhythm in an integrated way. The model is concentrated and hidden inside the *Modulator* object, making it easy to add new related aspects of rhythmic variation to a system. Data input can be taken from a stored musical representation or a live performance using appropriate electronic instrument interfaces. This is a design suitable to represent "interactive media": at all necessary points, algorithmically generated, stored, or human spontaneous input sources can be plugged in.

Finally, HCI concerns are better met using this pattern, because the *Customizer*, while being a separate object for architectural clarity, is nevertheless closely connected to the *Modulator*, i.e., the concept representation. This allows for richer, media-adequate interface metaphors to be implemented, so that the user can interact with the rhythmic concepts in a more meaningful way.

This pattern is easiest to implement if the underlying musical data model is based on discrete events—MUSICAL EVENTS (S4). . . .

**S3   IMPROVISATION HELPER **

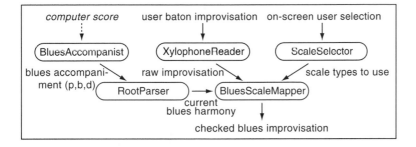

Figure 4.40: Improvisation support module in *WorldBeat*.

...you are developing an interactive music system that processes musical input in real time—BRANCHING TRANS-FORMER CHAIN (S1). Now you need to find a way to help the human players with their performance.

◇◇◇

Interactive music systems can support human players in new ways to avoid errors and create better music. However, such improvisation support must change incoming data in real time, and be flexible enough not to limit the human player too much.

The main goal of an interactive music system should not lie in mimicking traditional instruments, but rather in offering new conceptual instruments with semantically rich, interactive features not found in existing equipment. One of the most interesting new features possible is *intelligent player support:* the system lets the user play the creative part, but supports him with its musical knowledge, correcting small errors automatically.

Intelligent player support without stifling creativity

So as not to stifle creativity, however, the system should not influence or "correct" the player in more than one musical dimension. Since melodic or especially rhythmic corrections quickly lead to a loss of perceived immediacy for the player, the system should focus on a harmonic improvisation support: it should let the user play notes rhythmically free (play notes whenever he wishes), and melodically free (play high or low notes, runs, chords, etc.), but "fine-tune" the notes played so that they fit into the current harmonic context of the accompaniment.

Such improvisation support must be done carefully so as not to limit the player's creative freedom. Ideally, it would be adaptable to his level of expertise.

WorldBeat: Musical Design Patterns

In the *WorldBeat* system, such an improvisation support has been implemented in the *Musical Design Patterns* component. The *Accompanist* supplies the computer-generated accompaniment of a blues band (whose groove, etc. can be adjusted using other patterns such as the *MetricTransformer* described above). The *HarmonicAnalyser* uses a root-parsing algorithm as described in standard music literature to determine the current chord (say, Fm^7) in real time. The *InputAnalyser* offers a xylophone-like playing metaphor: the user makes downbeat gestures with the two infrared batons of the *WorldBeat* system in his hands. Gesture velocity determines volume, horizontal position determines pitch. The *Corrector* takes this input and maps it to the nearest, harmonically sound note in terms of the current accompaniment chord determined by the *HarmonicAnalyser*.

The result is quite fascinating: people who have never before played an instrument can walk up to the system and start improvising to a blues band—without playing wrong notes! This makes this *WorldBeat* component very attractive and popular among visitors who use the *WorldBeat* system. Experienced musicians can adjust the support to either a moderately hard to play, chromatic virtual xylophone using the batons (1 octave), or they can even use a full-scale electronic piano keyboard that can be added to the system at any time (7 octaves).

MusiKalscope

This pattern has also been applied independently in *MusiKalscope* [Fels et al., 1997], a system that lets the user improvise to bebop style jazz music and control a graphical feedback at the same time. The user plays a virtual drum pad using spatial trackers attached to his arms. The input is analysed by the *RhyMe* subsytem, and mapped to notes of a matching scale, depending on the current mode of the accompaniment. This mode, however, is determined in a separate a priori analysis process, which limits the flexibility of the system in terms of real time accompaniment input. The system also still lacks some reactiveness due to the input technology and metaphors.

Another application of the *ImprovisationHelper* pattern is our *NetMusic* scenario (see chapter 5). Here, the *Accompaniment* is not generated by the computer, but played by other humans. The real time *HarmonicAnalyser* ensures that even this situation, where the harmonic progressions to come may not even be known beforehand, can be covered using the *ImprovisationHelper* pattern.

NetMusic

Therefore:

Use the following combination of interacting software objects to create an *ImprovisationHelper*:

- **The *Accompanist* supplies the musical accompaniment, which can come from different sources (see examples).**

- **The *HarmonicAnalyser* constantly determines the current harmonic context (base and mode) delivered by the *Accompanist*, in real time.**

- **The *InputAnalyser* offers the user a musical interface to play his part in real time, and reads this user input, e.g., an improvisation to the accompaniment.**

- **The *Corrector* takes the "raw" musical input from the user, and the current harmonic situation from the *HarmonicAnalyser*, and adjusts the user input so that it fits into this harmonic context. Its output is a harmonically checked version of the original material played by the user.**

- **The *SupportAdaptor* offers the user a controller to decide how much improvisation support he wants. Experienced players can lower this to get more creative freedom (and responsibility for any wrong notes, of course).**

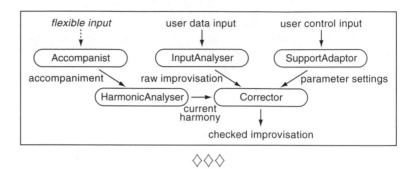

$\Diamond\Diamond\Diamond$

Avoid delays

The pattern makes a system simulate an "intelligent instrument". As such, interactivity is especially crucial in this pattern: if the delay between musical user input and corrected system output becomes noticeable (more than about 150 ms), users will lose the feeling of playing an instrument, and start thinking that they merely control some artificial music generator.

Fuzzy input

Also, the user interface should be designed so that input is not made in a too exact, but rather a slightly fuzzy way (not on an 88-key professional piano keyboard, for example). This helps to make the corrections of the system become hardly noticeable.

Advantages

For semantic modelling, this pattern is very valuable: it shows how a system can finally abstract from single notes, and let the user deal with higher-level concepts such as harmonic progressions, scales, etc.

Software engineering gets an interesting design in which the *HarmonicAnalyser* provides a class that does not depend on pre-recorded data to accomplish its task. This means that the system can use stored or live accompaniment if this pattern is applied. This is again a fundamental accomplishment necessary for a software architecture of interactive, new media: the data source, whether stored, computed, or provided in real time by a human, can be plugged into the system as desired.

HCI finally is rewarded with an exceptionally intriguing user interface metaphor that creates the impression of an intelligent instrument. The user can actually try out and influence the high-level semantic concepts inside the system, adjusting parameters such as the level of improvisation support, and then sending data (his own improvisation) into the system to hear the results.

Despite the abstraction from single notes that you can create for the user with this pattern, your implementation will nevertheless benefit from a representation of the underlying musical data that is easily manipulated on an event basis—MUSICAL EVENTS (S4). . . .

S4   MUSICAL EVENTS *

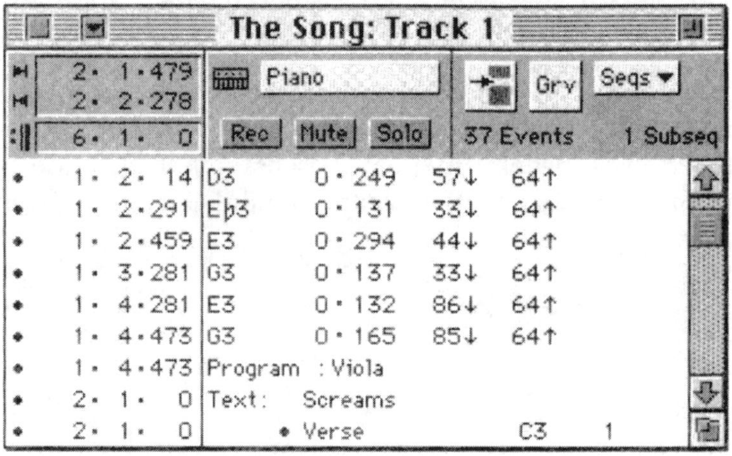

Figure 4.41: MIDI events in *Studio Vision Pro*.

. . . you are designing an interactive music system, and have decided how to do temporal adjustments—METRIC TRANS-FORMER (S2) and support spontaneous musical input—IMPROVISATION HELPER (S3). Now you need to decide on the form in which to store musical information.

◇◇◇

The most natural sound is created using originally recorded audio material. However, this representation does not offer any structural information about the musical material.

From music notation to MIDI

Historically, music has defined widely used representations that abstract from the actual sound, and instead represent music as a combination of musical events, or *notes*.

This concept was reinvented in the 1980s when synthesizers were only able to play one voice, but triggering several simultaneous sounds with only one key was a musical feature desired by the artists using such equipment. The result was the MIDI (Musical Instruments Digital Interface) standard [International MIDI Association, 1989], which defines not only an electrical interface but also a protocol to exchange musical information on the basis of "messages", which largely correspond to notes. For a more detailed treatment of MIDI, which is beyond the scope of this book, see the above specification.

Therefore:

Represent musical data in a form that abstracts from the audio signal, and that contains information about the beginning, end, sound, volume, and other performance aspects of each single note played.

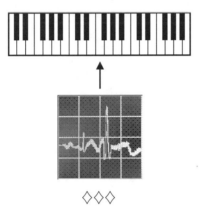

◇◇◇

This is a basic pattern that has no further references within this pattern language.

Chapter 5

Evaluation and Tool Support

"If we knew what it was we were doing,
it would not be called research, would it?"

—*Albert Einstein*

This chapter presents a number of evaluations of different aspects of the pattern-based framework presented. It first compares the framework with the set of initial requirements from chapter 2, then shows the results of a peer review of a sample pattern from the HCI design pattern language, and continues with a comparison of the approach and format used in this book to the recent definitions from a collaborative workshop on HCI design patterns. Subsequently, the systems that have resulted from using this approach are evaluated, and the use of the patterns presented in follow-up projects and education is addressed.

The chapter closes with a design sketch of a computer-based tool to author, review, and use pattern languages as presented in this book.

5.1 Comparison With Framework Requirements

Then pattern-based framework presented in this book compares as follows to the initial set of requirements (see p. 47):

- **Domain-independent, uniform, well-defined format.** Patterns were defined using a formal notation and a more extended discussion of the meaning of each component. This format has been followed successfully in the example languages, regardless of the domain.

- **Empirical evidence.** Not all example patterns contain references to published empirical studies strengthening their argument yet, but various patterns already include such information (see, for example, DYNAMIC DESCRIPTOR (H15)).

- **Domain-appropriate, design-supporting hierarchy.** The framework suggests a pattern hierarchy that reflects a top-down, unfolding design process. All example pattern languages exhibit this organization principle. The musical pattern language leads from patterns addressing the overall structure of a piece, down to patterns dealing with the characteristics of individual notes. The HCI pattern language starts with broad patterns about designing the overall user experience, leading to small-scale patterns about individual user interface objects. The software engineering patterns range from architectural concepts to implementation-oriented details.

- **Design dimension coverage.** The framework is general enough to allow additional design dimensions to be incorporated, depending on the domain. All pattern languages in the example actually use time as additional dimension to measure the "scale" of their patterns, and several patterns that address dynamic or sequential solutions also reflect this in some of their example media and storyboard-like sketches.

- **Lifecycle integration.** The framework takes Nielsen's *usability engineering lifecycle*, a widely known model of designing interactive systems, and illustrates how the various pattern languages can be used at each stage of this process model.

In all, unlike any of the previously existing efforts, the framework and sample pattern languages presented in this text basically fulfil all of the initial requirements. Improvements in various aspects are of course still possible.

5.2   Pattern Peer Review

An established method of judging the quality of academic publications is peer review by other experts in the field. To judge the soundness of pattern-related work, the software patterns community has established the *writers' workshop* procedure (see [Borchers, 2000a], or p. 38 for a summary of this method). This format has also been used successfully to evaluate HCI patterns [Borchers et al., 2001].

At the workshop *Pattern Languages For Interaction Design: Building Momentum* [Borchers et al., 2001], the pattern DOMAIN-APPROPRIATE DEVICES (H11) by the author, which is part of the HCI pattern language in the previous chapter, was reviewed by the following workshop participants, all of whom are also working in the field of HCI design patterns and have written patterns for this area:

Writers' workshop on DOMAIN-APPROPRIATE DEVICES

- Austin Henderson (Rivendel Consulting, California)

- Karri-Pekka Laakso (University of Helsinki, Finland)

- Victor Lombardi (Razorfish, New York)

- Carol Strohecker (Mitsubishi Electric Research Laboratory, Massachusetts)

- Yongmei Wu (Darmstadt University of Technology, Germany)

Since the pattern included in the language of this book has been improved as the result of this review, and since layout and references are slightly different, the original submitted pattern, as it was reviewed, is reproduced on the following pages.

10 DOMAIN-APPROPRIATE DEVICES *

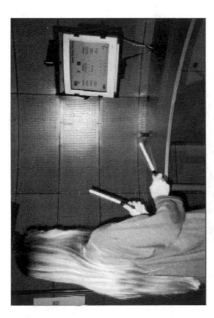

For a video example, see ⟨http://www.tk.uni-linz.ac.at/worldbeat/worldbeat.mov⟩.

Sample pattern for the CHI 20000 workshop "Pattern Languages for Interaction Design: Building Momentum" by Jan Borchers ⟨mailto:jan@tk.uni-linz.ac.at⟩.
Note: This pattern closely follows the Alexandrian format to examine how that format holds up for HCI patterns.

... you know what application area your interactive system is going to be about, and you have decided on the overall temporal and structural format of your interactive system—INCREMENTAL REVEALING (4), FLAT AND NARROW TREE (7). You are now ready to think about how the user should physically interact with your system at each phase.

◇◇◇

Modern interactive systems address a huge variety of application domains. Yet, they almost invariably use only mouse and keyboard as input devices.

Every interactive software system has a domain which it addresses and that its contents or functions are about. For example, a computer-based drawing course has the artistic domain of drawing as its application area, and a process control system in a power plant has the domain of that power plant and its functions as its application area.

However, most interactive systems use the standard keyboard and, nowadays, mouse as input devices, and nothing else. User interface designers put a lot of work into creating "metaphors" in which the virtual, on-screen world resembles items and concepts from the well-known, physical world. But all the while, those objects remain virtual, volatile images to be manipulated with the same, generic set of input devices and physical actions: type, point, click.

A reason that is commonly stated for this is that the development effort to create dedicated input devices is too high. But often, it is not even attempted to estimate the amount of extra work and its possible payoff, because it requires a lot of thinking from the designers to come up with new ideas apart from mouse and keyboard, and it is an area where products and standards are as comfortably developed and accessible as in the world of standard input devices.

But psychological research as well as common sense tell us that users are much more efficient, successful, and satisfied when they are offered input devices that resemble physical objects of the application domain. For example, Norman [1988, p. 23 ff.] talks in detail about the advantages of "natural mappings" from input device to system function, and gives a good example of a device perfectly designed for its dedicated purpose: a seat adjustment control in a car which is shaped like a miniature seat itself. To adjust his own seat, the user simply pushes the corresponding part of the miniature seat into the desired direction. It would have been far more cumbersome to understand and use the seat controls if they had been designed as a set of industry-standard buttons on the dashboard (and, if we imagine using those controls ourselves, it would probably also have been less fun).

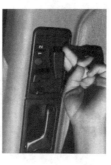

A domain-appropriate control to adjust a car seat.

The same is true for the *WorldBeat* system shown in the opening picture: It is an interactive exhibit that demonstrates to its users how computers open up new ways to interact with music, from conducting a computer orchestra, to improvising to a Blues band with computer support. While our initial designs included a standard keyboard and mouse as input devices, we

gradually found out that we did not really need them, and that they would spoil the "musical atmosphere" that the exhibit tries to create. The two infrared batons, on the other hand, are artefacts that resemble a conductor's baton, or xylophone sticks— objects that are well known from the musical domain. In taking them up, the user is already led away from thinking about interacting with a computer, into an experience of interacting with music. The system was elected one of the three most popular exhibits in the centre where it is installed [Borchers, 1997], and received an award for its new way to convey musical concepts.

Urp simulates wind between two physical building models.

Ishii and Ullmer [1997] developed the concept of *Tangible Bits* where the gap between human and computer is bridged by "coupling digital inormation to everyday physical objects and environments". For example, they created an *Urban Planning Workbench* (*Urp*) where buildings are represented by physical models that can be moved around on a map of the neighbourhood. Effects such as shadows and airflow are simulated in response to the physical placement of the objects and projected

onto the map. Informal studies showed that most architects who tried the system would use it immediately if available [Underkoffler and Ishii, 1999]. This is another example of the advantages of dedicated, application-specific input devices. Therefore:

Use input devices that resemble real objects from the application domain of your interactive system. Whenever users have to input something, determine whether the standard mouse and keyboard are really the best devices to use for this purpose, or if other devices can make working with the system more intuitive, efficient, and enjoyable.

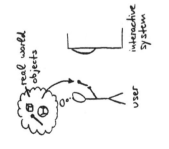

◇◇◇

A new device is also a good starting point to create a system that looks fresh, different, and intriguing—INNOVATIVE APPEARANCE (12), and that does not look like "a computer"—INVISIBLE HARDWARE (15). If your interactive system requires different forms of input, try to map them to your new input device—ONE INPUT DEVICE (20). . . .

References

Jan Borchers. WorldBeat: Designing a baton-based interface for an interactive music exhibit. In *Proceedings of the CHI 97 Conference on Human Factors in Computing Systems (Atlanta, GA, USA, March 22–27, 1997)*, pages 131–138, New York, 1997. ACM.

Hiroshi Ishii and Brygg Ullmer. Tangible bits: Towards seamless interfaces between people, bits and atoms. In *Proceedings of the CHI 97 Conference on Human Factors in Computing Systems (Atlanta, GA, USA, March 22–27, 1997)*, pages 234–241, New York, 1997. ACM.

Donald A. Norman. *The Psychology of Everyday Things*. Basic Books, New York, 1983.

John Underkoffler and Hiroshi Ishii. Urp: A luminous-tangible workbench for urban planning and design. In *Proceedings of the CHI 99 Conference on Human Factors in Computing Systems (Pittsburgh, PA, USA, May 15–20, 1999)*, pages 386–393, New York, 1999. ACM.

5

6

Results of Writers'
Workshop

The reviewing process is transcribed below, with the initials indicating the reviewer. The structure follows the format of a standard writers' workshop [Borchers, 2000a]. Remarks were usually agreed upon by the other reviewers, otherwise conflicting opinions are indicated.

5.2.1   Summary

The following statements were made by the reviewers to summarize the pattern.

- The pattern describes how to use alternative interaction devices, and gives real-world examples. (YW)

- The pattern recommends the use of matching input devices. (VL)

- The pattern indicates that the domain of application is critical to choosing the device. (AH)

5.2.2   Positive Formal Aspects

- The layout looks exactly like Alexander's patterns, which helps those familiar with Alexander's format to quickly find the important parts in this pattern. (AH)

- The problem and solution are easy to find; highlighting them using boldface works well. (YW, KL)

- The page size and column length are friendly to read. (VL)

- Title and photo introduce the pattern well. (VL)

- The rating helps reader to judge validity of pattern. (KL)

- The format uses implicit cues (typography, e.g. boldface) instead of explicit labels to indicate problem, solution, etc., which is good (repeated labels would be unaesthetic and boring). (VL, AH)

- Illustrations are frequent and distributed well across the text. (VL)

- The sketch echoes the opening photo, adding user's thoughts and being more abstract. (CS, YW)

- Several examples are included, and they are suitable (e.g., quotes from Norman). (KL)

- References are included. (CS)

5.2.3   Positive Contents Aspects

- The cover photo is very appropriate. (VL)

- The URL link to a "home page" for the opening example is a good idea. (VL)

- The amount of introductory context is well chosen. (VL)

- It is a good point that mouse and keyboard are often inappropriate. (KL)

- The car seat example is very well chosen. (AH)

- The solution includes "intuitive, efficient, and enjoyable" as system goals. (CS)

- The solution is well worded. (VL)

- The pattern includes links to other well-related patterns. (KL)

5.2.4   Format Improvement Suggestions

- The pattern may seem unstructured due to the lack of labels. (KL)—Response: The format is highly structured. (AH, CS)

- The structure becomes clear after reading the entire pattern, but a quick summary would be useful. (VL)

- There is an empty line missing before the word "Therefore" in the solution. (AH)

5.2.5   Contents Improvement Suggestions

- References suggest trying to map most interactions to the single input device if possible; this may not always be appropriate. (CS)*

- Modern interactive systems not only "address", but are even part of a variety of application domains. (AH)

- Mouse and keyboard should be left out of the problem statement to make it more timeless. (AH)

- Examples of when not to apply the pattern could be useful. (KL, AH)

- The title could be more specific. (VL)

- Is the pattern about both input and output devices? (AH)

- Leave out the notion of "modern" interactive systems, instead recommend choosing from the plethora of new input devices according to domain; as mobile devices, tangible bits, etc. become standard, this makes the pattern more timeless. (CS)

- The picture of URP could have close-up and whole, or a link to a video, or a photo series to make more self-explanatory. (AH, CS)

- Recommend to also choose actions (in addition to devices) from the real world (push real car seat to adjust it). (AH, KL)—Response: impossible for the Tangible Bits example. (CS)

- Include more in-depth discussion of *WorldBeat*, explaining what can be done with it (two sticks are not appropriate for conducting or selecting onscreen buttons). (CS, AH)*

(*) The comments marked with asterisks arise because this pattern was taken from a larger language, because the reviewers did not know that this language particularly addresses interactive exhibits, and because the text contains a detailed description of *WorldBeat* elsewhere.

5.2.6   Conclusion: Main Advantages

The Alexandrian form, the good page format, and the wording of problem and solution were regarded particularly positive form aspects. In the contents, the reviewers liked the well-chosen examples; the concept was seen as clearly being a pattern, and relating to other patterns.

5.3   Comparison With CHI 2000 Workshop Results

At the same CHI 2000 workshop on Pattern Languages for Interaction Design, the following definition was agreed upon by the participants:

> "An HCI design pattern captures the essence of a successful solution to a recurring usability problem in interactive systems."

CHI 2000: HCI design pattern definition

It went on to define which components constitute an HCI design pattern:

CHI 2000: HCI design pattern constituents

- name

- ranking

- sensitizing example

- context

- problem statement

- evidence (rationale, examples)

- solution

- sketch

- references (to other patterns)

- synopsis

- credits

Workshop confirms
approach

Both this definition and the list of pattern constituents very much confirm the validity of the approach and format used in this book: it contains all constituents from this list, apart from the synopsis, which is partly replaced by a graphical representation of the patterns hierarchy, and the credits, which are obvious since the patterns are part of this text.

DOMAIN-
APPROPRIATE
DEVICES used as
workshop sample
pattern

In fact, as a consequence of these similarities, the pattern DOMAIN-APPROPRIATE DEVICES (H11) reviewed above was used as an example of an HCI design pattern on the official workshop poster presented at CHI 2000 [Borchers et al., 2001].

5.4   Evaluation of a Resulting System: *WorldBeat*

To judge the validity of a method such as the pattern framework described in this text, it is helpful to have a look at the resulting systems that have been implemented using the approach.

The pattern-based approach was first considered during user interface and software design of the *WorldBeat* exhibit. Even though the pattern languages presented in this book did not exist in their entirety yet when *WorldBeat* design started, the idea to wrap knowledge from the application domain (music in this case) into pattern form was one of its initial design goals. This is particularly true for its *Musical Design Patterns* component (see below). More patterns, including those for HCI and software design, emerged during the design of this system.

To better understand how this exhibit used patterns in its design, its overall architecture and features are outlined here.

5.4.1 Project Background

WorldBeat is an interactive music exhibit that was designed for the *KnowledgeNet* floor of the *Ars Electronica Center (AEC).*

The AEC is a technology "museum of the future" [Janko et al., 1996], demonstrating to the general public how information technology will change the way we live, work, learn, relax, and communicate in the next century. It opened in Linz, Austria, in September 1996. The centre consists of five floors, each addressing a different aspect of life - from a 3-D *CAVE* in the basement that lets users experience virtual realities with a focus on entertainment and scientific visualization, to the *Sky Media Loft* café on the third floor with a focus on personal and Internet communication.

Ars Electronica Center

Its second floor, *KnowledgeNet,* focuses on aspects of computer use in learning and working environments. It was designed and equipped by our Telecooperation Research Group at Linz University. It consists of a *Class/Conference Room of the Future* [Mühlhäuser et al., 1996], demonstrating the use of group support systems, teleconferencing technology, interactive whiteboards, etc., and an area with *World-Beat* and other individual exhibits that deal with certain subject areas such as new media, new user interfaces, or new learning approaches, in more depth.

KnowledgeNet floor

The entire floor was designed to convey the message that careful use of information technology can make learning a more *active, cooperative,* and *motivating* experience. Naturally, this also had a strong influence on the design of the *WorldBeat* user experience.

5.4.2   System Features

WorldBeat: New ways of interacting with music

WorldBeat was designed to show AEC visitors new ways of interacting with music with computer support. Consequently, the entire exhibit is controlled using just a pair of infrared batons. This fulfilled our goals of creating a consistent way to control the exhibit, and of creating an innovative, appearance to attract visitors. It also led to a non-technical look, which avoids scaring off computer novices, and resulted in an input device that was much more appropriate for the domain "music" than standard mouse and keyboard, but without intimidating visitors with a professional music keyboard or similar instrumental interface. Both batons are used for musical input in the various modules described below, with the right baton doubling as pointing device to select features on-screen.

The following software modules were designed and implemented for *WorldBeat* to demonstrate new ways of computer-supported interaction with music:

WorldBeat features

- The *Virtual Baton* module enables the visitor to conduct a piece of music. It shows that a computer system can play back a stored score while leaving (rhythmic and dynamic) control over the actual performance to the user.

- In the *Query By Humming* module, visitors hum the beginning of a song, and the computer locates the complete piece in its database. This demonstrates how computers can simulate human musical recognition processes.

- With the *Musical Memory* module, visitors can test how good they are at recognizing instruments through their sounds alone. It is an example of a game-like courseware to learn about music.

- In the *NetMusic* module, visitors can play together with partners over the Internet. It demonstrates the cooperative possibilities of computer-based learning environments.

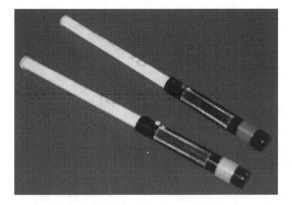

Figure 5.1: The *Lightning II* infrared batons by Buchla and Associates.

- Finally, using the *Musical Design Patterns* module, users can change basic parameters of musical improvisation and performance "patterns", e.g., the "groove" (swing) in a blues piece, and they can even improvise to the music without playing wrong notes. This module shows that computers can offer a completely new way of creating music that can be attractive and rewarding to all players, regardless of their prior musical knowledge and abilities.

5.4.3   Implementation

The *WorldBeat* exhibit runs on an Apple Power Macintosh® 8500/120 or higher computer. A Musical Instruments Digital Interface (MIDI) interface connects it to a *Buchla Lightning II* spatial MIDI controller [Rich, 1996] that consists of two wireless, infrared *batons* (see Fig. 5.1), a *tracker unit* that we attached to the computer monitor, and the *base unit* that contains the controller interface and MIDI sound module. The batons are battery-operated, and each features an additional action button.The exhibit further consists of a microphone connected to a Roland pitch-to-MIDI converter (for *Query By Humming*), and standard audio equipment (amplifier, tape deck, speakers, and headphones).

WorldBeat:
MIDI-based

We developed the *WorldBeat* software using the *MAX* multimedia programming environment [Dobrian, 1995] by Opcode Inc., a development system especially for applications that process MIDI data in real time. *MAX* supports visual programming for most standard tasks. Applications are created as a hierarchical network of *patches* that each process data (usually MIDI messages) in a certain way. We extended *MAX* by implementing new patch types, for example to manage the graphical user interface of *WorldBeat*.

The idea to use the infrared batons as navigational devices resulted in the following data flow in the *WorldBeat* system:

WorldBeat data flow

- The visitor stands in front of the exhibit (see the figure on p. 133), looking at the large display, and gestures with the two batons in her hands. Each baton contains infrared light-emitting diodes that continuously emit signals in all directions. Special signals are sent when the action button on a baton is pressed or released.

- The infrared tracker, mounted directly below the monitor, measures the angles at which it receives the signals from the two batons, and converts these into horizontal and vertical position data with a resolution of 128 steps in each dimension. It also uses the button press/release events sent from the batons to determine the current button states. This results in a stream of tuples $(x_1, y_1, b_1, x_2, y_2, b_2)$ being sent to the Lightning base unit, with coordinates $x_i, y_i \in \{0, ..., 127\}$ and button flags $b_i \in \{0, 1\}$.

- The base unit converts those tuples into MIDI messages that imitate four continuous and two discrete MIDI controllers, and sends those out to its MIDI port. The unit also contains basic gesture recognition which its presets use to directly create MIDI notes from downward "beat" gestures. This is used by *WorldBeat* modules that just require the user to play a virtual instrument with the batons in a drumstick-like fashion.

- In the more advanced *WorldBeat* modules, the MIDI controller data is sent via the MIDI interface to the Macintosh serial port, where it is picked up by the *WorldBeat* system and interpreted in several ways: the interface manager computes the cursor position on the screen depending on the position of the right baton, and the currently selected *WorldBeat* component usually uses the data to perform other actions.

- All resulting events that describe MIDI playing messages are finally sent back from the Macintosh via the MIDI interface to the Lightning base unit. It contains a sound card with sampled instrument sounds that follow the *GM (General MIDI)* standard for MIDI instrument setups. The base unit creates the requested audio signals, which are then sent to the amplifier and loudspeakers, tape deck, or headphones.

5.4.4   Usage Scenario

To explain how the visitor actually interacts with the system, the following section describes the interaction metaphors used in each module.

Interaction
metaphors:

When walking up to the exhibit, the visitor first gets a short on-screen explanation how to *navigate* with the batons. Since the Lightning system features two batons, we established the convention that the right baton is always used for navigation, i.e., replacing the mouse. The visitor simply points at the screen where a yellow spot shows the current cursor position, and presses the action button to select something.

Navigation

Playing virtual instruments in the *Joy-Sticks* module uses metaphors that are built into the Lightning hardware and depend on the instrument type. Instruments that are played with one or two *mallets* (including drum kits, xylophones and similar instruments) use a natural mapping: downward beat gestures play the instrument(s) in a velocity-sensitive way. With *chordal* instruments, either

Playing instruments

two-finger operation is employed (as in one of the piano settings), or a number of fixed chords are placed into 2-D space and can be triggered by beat gestures at their position (as in a guitar setup). Finally, instruments that in reality require some different action to play a note (like wind-instruments) are simulated using the *action button* on the baton to play a note, and the 2-D baton position information to control pitch and velocity simultaneously.

Conducting

Conducting a piece in the *Virtual Baton* module uses a more refined gesture recognition than the one built into Lightning, to give exact control over the playback speed and dynamics of a classical piece. The software tracks the right baton, concentrating on vertical movement only, and plays the next beat each time it detects a change from downward to upward movement. Gesture size determines playback volume. The original algorithm was developed by a group of computer music professionals [Lee et al., 1992]; we adapted it to be usable by normal visitors, and integrated it into *WorldBeat*.

Improvisation

Improvising in the *Musical Design Patterns* module finally uses a new musical interaction metaphor: the visitor again plays with downbeat gestures on an "invisible xylophone" in front of him. The actual notes that are mapped onto the "keys" of this xylophone, however, are constantly recomputed by the system to fit into the current harmonic context of the accompaniment. That way, the user has complete control over rhythm and melodic shape of his performance, while the system modifies his input with its own harmonic knowledge to create an aesthetically pleasing result. For musical experts, this support can be switched off, showing the adaptability of the system to different user experience levels.

Wrapping musical patterns into software and user interface objects

This last component also included the first examples of the pattern principle: various musical concepts and aspects of the playing style of the accompanying blues band were modelled by groups of interacting software objects, and equipped with a user interface that allowed users to experiment with those concepts and understand them by interacting with them. Some examples are:

- The TRIPLET GROOVE (M9) playing pattern of the accompanying band was made accessible through an on-screen slider. While the band is playing, visitors can change the timing of this accompaniment.

- The degree of freedom given to the bass player in conctructing a bass line can be adjusted interactively, or a standard WALKING BASS (M10) pattern can be activated.

- For improvisation, visitors can choose between a virtual vibraphone containing only a PENTATONIC SCALE (M7) plus BLUE NOTES (M8), or a full chromatic version.

In all modules, we supplied a visual interface designed in cooperation with a graphic artist that allows the user to navigate through the functions easily and supports them with brief online descriptions of the current metaphor and features.

A more detailed storyboard of a typical interaction with *WorldBeat* is given in appendix B.

Sample run in appendix

5.4.5 Evaluation

Four types of evaluation took place in developing the *WorldBeat* system and its user interface: during the design phase, we continuously had novice users have a look at our interface and had them use the exhibit modules that were already working. As a result, we redesigned and improved navigation and visual appearance several times.

Iterative prototyping

During the opening week of the AEC, the author spent five days at the exhibit, demonstrating its use to visitors and receiving direct feedback, but also observing users and recording interaction problems and common errors. This showed that using the batons for navigation and playing

Positive feedback from observations

posed no problems to users, although some details such as the exact conducting movement, and the fact that most users would not read lengthy instructions, required us to redesign the online help.

Musical Design Patterns most successful

Improvising in the *Musical Design Patterns* module turned out to be the most attractive component. Users enjoyed "jamming" with a blues band without playing wrong notes. This module appeared to have found the right balance between free user input and system guidance. With freedom in rhythm and melodic shape, nobody cared that the keyboard constantly changes to offer a matching scale.

Patterns helped understanding musical concepts

It also showed that modelling musical concepts as "patterns", by turning them into software objects with an appropriate user interface, helped visitors greatly to understand those principles. For example, it was frequently observed that visitors quickly grasped the concept of groove in jazz, by playing with the on-screen groove slider for a few seconds. It usually takes the author much longer to explain this concept to musical amateurs without the help of such an interactive tool.

Formal survey: Good marks for *WorldBeat*

After the opening week, the AEC conducted a survey among visitors. Each of the 13 major exhibits was given a grade from 1 ("very easy to understand, very interesting") to 5 ("very complicated to understand, very uninteresting"). The 104 participants gave *WorldBeat* an average grade of $\mu = 2.08$, i.e., the second best grade possible, with a standard deviation of $\sigma = 1.12$.

WorldBeat top 3 exhibit

The participants were also asked to list their three favourite exhibits. Here, *WorldBeat* reached the third position, with 13.5% of the participants listing it in their "Top Three" list. Only the two million-dollar virtual reality installations in the AEC—the 3-D Cave, and a VR flight simulator—were listed more often than *WorldBeat*, whose hardware can be purchased for around US$15,000.

Multimedia Transfer Award winner

Finally, *WorldBeat* was submitted to the 1998 *Multimedia Transfer* competition, which has the goal of honouring academic software projects that show an outstanding success

of transferring research ideas into concrete systems. Selected in a two-phase competition from among 160 submis-
sions coming from academic institutions throughout Germany, Austria, and Switzerland, *WorldBeat* became one of
the nine *Multimedia Transfer Award* winners.

Since then, the system has been demonstrated to the public   Permanent exhibit
on many occasions. It remained a permanent exhibit in the
Ars Electronica Center for four years from 1996 until 2000,
and was exhibited at other locations, such as the *Techniek
Museum* in Delft, The Netherlands, for most of 1998.

Details about the design of the *WorldBeat* system, particularly its user interface design and evaluation, can be found
in [Borchers, 1997], and in the video proceedings of that
conference. The video, as well as additional material about   *WorldBeat*
the system, is also available online on the *actibits* home page   demonstration video
(see appendix A).

5.5   Reusing Patterns

The languages created during the design of *WorldBeat* were
reused and refined in a series of follow-up projects.

5.5.1   The *Interactive Fugue*

In the *Interactive Fugue* project, the author worked with a   *Interactive Fugue:*
graduate student to develop an interactive exhibit about   Completely
Johann Sebastian Bach's classical fugue style of composi-   pattern-based design
tion. In the final system, users can record their own fugue
motif, create a simple fugue from this material, and learn
about the structure of this musical style in the process (see
Fig. 5.2). The system uses a baton-based interface similar to
WorldBeat for input.

This project was initiated to prove the validity of the
pattern-based approach presented in this book. Therefore,
its entire design process, from requirements analysis to implementation, was based on this pattern format.

Figure 5.2: Opening screen of the *Interactive Fugue* exhibit, offering the user to listen to some classical fugue pieces, compose their own fugue, or hear other visitors' compositions. Additional information about Bach is available via his portrait.

HCI patterns helped reuse experience

For this project, 15 HCI patterns from the languages of the author, as well as from the collection by Tidwell [1998], and several new patterns were used to inform the user interface design. Here, the pattern format proved particularly useful to carry over experience from the earlier *WorldBeat* project to this new effort.

Application domain patterns supported communicating with expert

Moreover, the application domain (classical fugue composition) was discussed with a music teacher and expert in this field, who helped us to model the fundamental concepts as a language of 16 patterns for fugue composition, which is also included in [Dannenberg, 1999]. The music expert was quick to understand the pattern format, agreed to its general appropriateness for this field, and was able to discuss musical issues using this approach quite well.

Software patterns informed software development

The project also made use of several software patterns that were partly adopted from the "Gang of Four" book

[Gamma et al., 1995], such as the FAÇADE pattern to hide different subsystem interfaces behind a common interface, and partly developed originally. These altogether 11 patterns are also included in the above Master's thesis.

5.5.2 *Personal Orchestra* and *Virtual Vienna*

The most current projects that served both to use the existing pattern languages, and to refine them, are two interactive exhibits designed by the author for the HOUSE OF MUSIC VIENNA (see appendix A for the URL), a large exhibition centre in the heart of Vienna that lets visitors explore the rich musical history, present, and future of the city.

HOUSE OF
MUSIC VIENNA

The first exhibit, *Personal Orchestra*, lets visitors conduct a large video and audio rendition of the Vienna Philharmonic orchestra. The material was custom-recorded by us in the Golden Hall, where the orchestra traditionally give their New Year's concert that is broadcast worldwide. Visitors use the infrared baton technology to control not just volume, but also the exact speed of the orchestra playing, as well as the emphasis on individual orchestra sections, through conducting gestures in real time. The system builds on our experience with the *WorldBeat* conducting feature, but adds a video display of the orchestra, and uses original digital audio material instead of artificial MIDI sound generation for audio. Successful conducting is rewarded with a digital photo of the visitor in front of "his" orchestra.

Personal Orchestra

The second system, *Virtual Vienna*, is a virtual reality city tour of Vienna, focusing on places that are important from a music-historical point of view. It uses a large display and spatial audio to immerse visitors in a photorealistic panorama view of a place within the city. Users can move around in this panorama using a custom-designed *NaviPad* with three degrees of freedom, and change to other places either using hot spot links within the panorama, or by choosing a place from a map that is shown on a separate

Virtual Vienna

display integrated into the *NaviPad*. Information about objects of particular interest is available through hot spot links within the panorama that lead to short descriptive pages with text and graphics about the object in question.

At the time of writing, our formal user studies to evaluate the final systems are yet to be finished. However, the exhibits have generated very positive feedback already. In particular, the HOUSE OF MUSIC VIENNA recently judged the *Personal Orchestra* system to be its most attractive exhibit.

The HCI design patterns presented in this book were used during the development process. The HCI pattern language for interactive exhibits was passed on to the customer, and in subsequent design meetings, it helped tremendously to quickly explain and discuss design decisions.

Using HCI patterns in customer communication

As an example, at one of these meetings for *Virtual Vienna*, the customer suggested that several exhibits with standard monitors be installed instead of one exhibit with a large projection. The idea was to lower the cost for display hardware and increase visitor throughput. However, after pointing out that this idea would violate several of the HCI design patterns presented, particularly IMMERSIVE DISPLAY (H13) and COOPERATIVE EXPERIENCE (H3), the idea was withdrawn in favour of the single larger exhibit. Sound on this system was also made optional, and provisions for several headsets were installed, to avoid interference with the ATTRACTION SPACE (H2) of the neighbouring *Personal Orchestra* exhibit.

Using HCI patterns in developer communication

During meetings and written communication, not only with the customer, but also with the software development group, being able to point to the HCI patterns saved significant time that would otherwise have been spent on repeatedly explaining the importance of the respective concepts and their rationale from past projects. The concise and easily remembered pattern names especially were extremely valuable in this context, and helped to create a common vocabulary within the entire design team.

5.6 Study of Didactic Usefulness

An important claim made by this work is that the HCI pattern format is a form suitable not only to capture design experience for follow-up projects, but also to introduce new designers to important HCI design concepts, and to use this form as a teaching aid in HCI design courses.

During an HCI design course for first-year computer science undergraduates in the summer 1999 term, the author spent one lecture of 90 minutes altogether dealing with HCI patterns: the idea of patterns, their origin in architecture, and their use for capturing HCI design concepts were explained, and copies of Jenifer Tidwell's *Common Ground* HCI pattern collection handed out. Students then took about 15 minutes to study the collection, and to find patterns that they could relate to their first own user interface prototyping exercise on which they were working at that time.

Using HCI patterns in a course

Informal feedback during this exercise, and in the following week while the prototypes were finished, was very encouraging. Most students were able to immediately relate several patterns to problems they had been facing during their design themselves.

Positive informal feedback

This was confirmed in a formal statistical evaluation, which was carried out two weeks after the above lecture, in an unannounced lecture evaluation. Students were asked to rate various aspects of the lecture, including the following questions concerning the design pattern approach presented:

Formal survey

1. I remember the following HCI design patterns:

2. For the overall understanding and remembering of user interface design concepts, the patterns were (1=very useful ... 5=completely useless).

3. I was able to find problems and solutions for our own design project in the pattern collection (1=absolutely ... 5=not at all).

4. I can imagine using this pattern concept in future design projects (1=certainly yes ... 5=certainly not).

Results and Discussion

$n_0 = 32$ students filled out the questionnaire; of these, $n = 26$ answered the questions about patterns. The results are shown in Fig. 5.3.

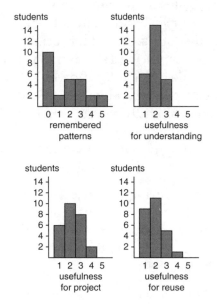

Figure 5.3: Results of the patterns survey, showing how many patterns were remembered, and their perceived usefulness for learning, current work, and future projects.

Students remember
patterns

On average, $\mu \approx 1.73$ patterns were remembered, with a standard deviation of $\sigma \approx 1.65$. Lecturers will agree that this is quite promising, considering that students only spent relatively short time with the material during the lecture, only looking at a few patterns in any detail, and that the material had not been revisited by students for the final examinations yet. The vocabulary function of HCI design patterns seems to have succeeded quite well. The large standard deviation reflects the fact that several students wrote down no patterns at all, an effect that does not fit into the standard distribution; with an examination-like test situation, they may have spent more time trying to remember some of the patterns.

The usefulness of the pattern language for understanding HCI design issues was rated with an overall $\mu \approx 1.96$, i.e., with the second-best grade possible, with a relatively small standard deviation of $\sigma \approx 0.65$, indicating a high level of consensus among the students.

Students consider HCI patterns useful

Usefulness for current project work was rated slightly worse, but still with an overall second best grade ($\mu \approx 2.23$). A slightly higher standard deviation ($\sigma \approx 0.89$) shows that there was less consensus on this question.

Finally, the confidence that this pattern concept would be reused in future projects was again quite high ($\mu \approx 1.94$), with relatively great consensus ($\sigma \approx 0.81$).

In all, these results indicate that a pattern approach in HCI education is useful and convincing. Through the structured combination of widely known examples with generalized recommendations, even first-year undergraduates can quickly relate to this format, and find it useful and worth considering for their further projects.

5.7 Publishing Peer Review

A final indication that the method and patterns presented in this book are sound is the fact that, based upon initial feedback from several experts in the field who reviewed a late draft, two major international computer science publishers have expressed in writing their intent to publish this work as part of their programme.

Positive expert reviews for publishing

5.8 PET: A Pattern Editing Tool

One of the main reasons stated for the formal model of pat-

From formal model to hypertext

tern languages as presented in chapter 3 was the possibility of building an authoring and browsing system to write, read, and browse a pattern language. This formal model defines a pattern language in a way that makes it quite straightforward to represent it as a hypertext:

- The pattern language is stored as a graph with patterns as nodes, and the references between patterns as directed edges, or links.

- Each pattern node consists of a sequence of *contents blocks* for name, ranking, sensitizing example, context, problem statement, several existing examples, solution, diagram, and references. Each content block is a multimedia container for text, graphics and/or other media types.

- The context and references blocks contain bidirectional links to other patterns within their textual section.

Sample pattern languages highly structured

The pattern languages presented in this book, while written as readable texts without disturbing explicit text tags for each pattern component, nevertheless follow the formal definition exactly, and are therefore highly structured through implicit, typographical rules. Inserting these patterns into a hypertext environment is therefore an easy task (see Fig. 5.4 below).

Existing systems

Numerous systems exist that try to make design patterns and guidelines accessible with computer support (see, e.g., [Alben et al., 1994]), and at the CHI 2000 workshop, an initiative was founded by Trætteberg and Welie [H:Trætteberg00] that has created an online repository of HCI design patterns, together with some means of adding review comments to these patterns.

PET

The following sections show the requirements analysis for such a tool, and present the design and a prototype of a possible system, the Pattern Editing Tool PET.

Target Group

The system is supposed to represent pattern languages independently of their domain. This means that typical users
are HCI designers and software engineers, but also user
representatives and experts from the application domain
of an interactive software design project. Moreover, interdisciplinary use as outlined in the approach in this book
will lead to people frequently browsing pattern languages
in whose domain they are not themselves trained profes-
sionally.

Interdisciplinary use

Tasks and Scenarios

Independently of their professional background, users fall
into three categories according to the main task they may
wish to perform in relation to a pattern language: they may
be *authoring* and creating it, they may act as peer *reviewers* of
an existing collection, or they may be *using* it with the goal
of applying the patterns to their current design problems,
or to learn about a design field in general. Only the latter activity, though, will normally include users from other
professions.

*Authoring, reviewing,
and reading*

Typical sample scenarios are the following:

1. An HCI design practitioner needs to design an interactive exhibit, a field that he has not worked in before.
   He would like to find out what to look out for in interactive exhibit UI design. He will therefore be interested to get a quick overview of an existing HCI pattern language on the subject, and he will also want to
   find entries quickly via a keyword or full-text search.

2. A software engineer with some interest in research
   has been asked to peer-review a pattern collection
   written by a colleague, in the fashion of a writer's
   workshop. She will want to be able to browse the collection for overview, and to read individual patterns

on-screen or as printout, and will need to add comments to each pattern as suggested by the workshop procedure.

3. A domain expert about music has been asked to formulate his expertise as a set of patterns about classical music composition. He would like to write the body text with his favourite word processor, then convert it and add audio or score examples to the material for clarification.

Design: Features and Constraints

PET features

The above scenarios lead to an initial conceptual design of the PET system that includes the following functionalities, in order of importance:

- creating, annotating, and reading pattern texts;

- including multimedia examples, such as audio and video clips, or diagrams and photos, as well as links to other patterns;

- creating an intuitive, graphical overview of the existing pattern hierarchy;

- providing quick access to patterns via keyword or full text search;

- offering a sequential way to navigate around the language and print patterns.

In addition, the system should fulfil some constraints that help its widespread use:

- It should not require explicit installation of some specific application software or the use of a specific operating system.

- It should allow for links to other patterns and pattern languages via internet standards.

- It should base the content format on widely accepted, open standards for maximum accessibility.

Design: Architecture

The above requirements can be met by a system architecture that uses a document format based on an Extensible Markup Language (XML) structure definition. A first such specification for user interface design patterns was developed by van Welie [2000]. By applying the formal definition from this book to that XML model, it was possible to improve the modelling of links between patterns.

PET: XML-based

However, it would be unwise to force a single "correct" pattern structure definition onto authors, since many may already have produced patterns that they will be reluctant to rewrite, and also because the structure put forward here will not always be the best to use. Therefore, the system should merely suggest the use of that structure, but allow for the inclusion of additional pattern document classes, with different levels of formal structuring. A minimum pattern format, for example, could simply be defined as a monolithic text document that does not include any additional external information about its inner structure.

Pattern documents can then be displayed in an XML-capable web browser window. Additional functionality, such as the graphical overview, is supplied via Java applets.

Each pattern is then accessible via a URL of the corresponding document. More detailed references can point to individual content blocks (components) of a pattern.

The authoring of individual contents blocks is best left to existing specialized tools. It would be unwise to try and force an "integrated pattern writer's environment" complete with editors for all sorts of media types onto pattern authors, since work practices, systems used, media types, and personal preferences for content creation are highly varied.

Interface to existing tools

Instead, the system should allow the author to hook his pre-
pared content blocks into the pattern language, and support arranging, reviewing, and browsing this growing collection.

Storyboard of Sample Implementation

This section describes a sample interaction with PET, and
gives a few screenshots that show how the system can be
implemented.

Creating a pattern

An author prepares his pattern content blocks in XML format with his favourite authoring tools, using a document
definition of the pattern form used in this book, or a different one that is more suitable for his pattern format. He links
those content blocks into PET by specifying the base URL of
the pattern. PET parses the pattern document, and displays
it in a structured form that makes the various components
clearly recognizable (see Fig. 5.4). Problem and solution,
the central components of each pattern, are emphasized visually to support quick visual scanning.

Multimedia and
cross-reference links

The user can customize this display by hiding or showing
each pattern contents block, a setting that is retained when
switching to a different pattern. Text and graphics are displayed directly, while audio and video samples can be activated by selecting their icon representations within the pattern contents block.

Linear navigation
support

Links inside the context and reference sections of each pattern also lead to the respective target pattern. In addition, PET offers a breadth-first-search sequential navigation
metaphor through the entire language via "next" and "previous" buttons, for those who prefer to read a language
from beginning to end. This navigation metaphor also defines the contents structure that PET uses to print the language for easier sustained reading. File handling, printing,
and searching menus are not shown, for the sake of clarity.

Language graph
display, and quick
help

As more patterns are created, PET automatically builds and
updates a graphical representation of the pattern hierarchy

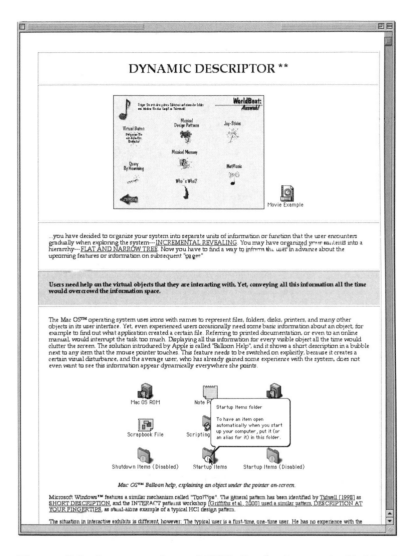

Figure 5.4: A screen shot of PET displaying an individual HCI design pattern.

as a whole (see Fig. 5.5), which uses a semi-automatic layout algorithm and can be displayed separately, or next to the current pattern. The author, as well as the reader later on, can jump to patterns by selecting them from this graphical overview. The solution statement from each pattern is displayed as a short help text when the user moves the cursor over a pattern, so he can see what the pattern is about before jumping to it. (This feature uses the DYNAMIC DE-SCRIPTOR pattern from chapter 4.)

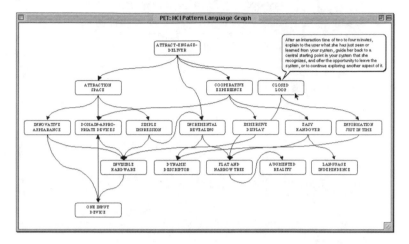

Figure 5.5: PET displaying an entire HCI pattern language graph. Moving the cursor over a pattern pops up its solution statement as a quick help text.

Adding reviewer's comments

Reviewing in the form of the *Writer's Workshop* presented in chapter 2, and exemplified earlier in this chapter, strongly depends on the social interaction of the reviewers. Nevertheless, it makes sense to collect comparable comments from reviewers who access the pattern online, alone or in a group. For reviewing, PET therefore offers a way to add comments to each pattern contents block. PET requires the reviewer to classify each comment. It distinguishes between positive comments, and suggestions for improvement, each for both formal aspects and contents aspects, as well as summary statements.

As presented here, PET is just an initial iteration in the design of a suitable support tool, and serves as proof of concept to show that such support is feasible.

This concludes the evaluation of the approach presented in this book, and the discussion of tool support for such a framework.

Chapter 6

Summary and Further Research

"Mit Eifer hab' ich mich der Studien beflissen;
Zwar weiß ich viel, doch möcht' ich alles wissen."

—*J. W. von Goethe: Faust*

This chapter will briefly sketch the motivation for this work, and then summarize its main original contributions to the research field of HCI design patterns.

6.1 Motivation

The quality of a user interface is crucial to the success of interactive systems. Good user interface design, however, requires experts from human–computer interaction, software engineering, and the application domain of a software project to collaborate in an interdisciplinary design team. Communication between these disciplines is often difficult, as is capturing their design experience for follow-up projects, corporate memory, training and education. This work has suggested a new pattern-based framework for tackling these problems.

Motivation: Improving interdisciplinary cooperative user experience design

6.2   Main Contributions

Contributions:

To this end, the first contribution of this work is a comprehensive introduction to the concept of patterns as introduced in the 1970s by the architect Christopher Alexander, who defined pattern languages as hierarchies of textual descriptions of successful solutions to recurring design problems in urban architecture.

HCI patterns history
and research survey

This is followed by an overview of how the idea has been adopted by software engineering, and an exhaustive survey of the history and state of the art in the field of design patterns in human–computer interaction. It includes interesting findings on early references to Alexander's work by major HCI texts that previously have generally been overlooked, and outlines the results of all known workshops, as well as most individual efforts, on the subject that have begun to evolve since the HCI pattern movement has gained momentum around 1997.

Participation in HCI
patterns discussion
and definition

The author has also actively participated in, and to some degree organized, the discussion and definition process in the still relatively small, but very active and now quickly growing, HCI patterns research community. He was a member of the first workshop on interaction patterns held at a conference from the PLoP (Pattern Languages of Programming) series at ChiliPLoP 1999, connecting as an HCI researcher to people from the software engineering patterns community, and authored the resulting report [Borchers, 2000a].

Workshop initiatives

The next two pattern workshops at major HCI conferences, INTERACT'99 and CHI 2000, were co-organized by the author. The latter event in particular included virtually all individuals who had been doing major research in the HCI patterns field. These workshops and their reports have led to an increased visibility of this field within HCI and software engineering, and iteratively improved basic concepts such as a definition of HCI pattern languages, their goals, structure, and contents. These contributions are reflected in this work, although they were mostly included in the survey section for sake of clarity.

Another significant contribution of this work is the formal specification of the structure of a pattern language, which is independent of the domain that the language may address. The definition is refined by a detailed discussion of the meaning of the individual pattern constituents and their composition. It should be kept in mind at this point that these "languages" are not programming languages, but rather hierarchies of patterns, which are textual descriptions of successful design solutions.

Formal pattern language definition

The definition has been used to apply the pattern concept not only to HCI, but also to software engineering and particularly the application domain of software projects. While there is a large body of work available about software patterns, applying the principle to the application domain of an interactive software design process has only been undertaken by few research projects.

Application domain patterns

In particular, the present work is the first to suggest a cross-disciplinary method to use patterns in the design process of interactive systems in a structured and uniform way. The method is embedded into a widely known model of usability engineering, making it more practical for application.

Interdisciplinary, uniform, embedded approach

The languages contained in this book not only serve as proof of the soundness of the pattern-based approach, but also stand as original contributions in their own right. The HCI pattern language is the most comprehensive, and captures crucial design help for the growing field of interactive exhibits. It is important to see that with the advent of public information kiosks, more playful desktop software, and the World-Wide Web, the need for exhibit-like design primarily for first-time and one-time users with short interaction times has spread far beyond the obvious museum scenario.

HCI pattern language (not only) for interactive exhibits

The musical pattern language illustrates how to capture knowledge from the application domain of a project, but also represents the first time such knowledge has been gathered, structured, and presented in this format.

Musical application domain pattern language

The software design patterns capture some of the tech-

Software patterns for interactive music systems

niques used by the author in building interactive music systems.

PET

To illustrate the feasibility of computer tool support for working with pattern languages, the Pattern Editing Tool PET, a prototypical software environment, was designed, based on an initial analysis of target groups, their tasks, and typical usage scenarios.

Finally, many of the systems implemented as part of this work represent important contributions. The award-winning *WorldBeat* exhibit shows how computer support can open up entirely new ways of interacting with musical data. It gives a glimpse of the future in which home users, for example, may be able to hum the first notes of a symphony to start its playback from their audio equipment, then pick up a baton and not only conduct with the music but actually control the orchestra. It also shows that some musical patterns can be cast directly into software structures with an appropriate user interface, enabling users to learn about musical concepts by interacting with them. Subsequent exhibits such as *Personal Orchestra* have extended the degree of realism in musical interaction, while others, such as the *Interactive Fugue* and *Virtual Vienna,* have shown the more general validity of the pattern-based approach, and particularly the HCI design pattern language developed.

Systems show importance of user interface for utilizing new media technologies

But above all, they have shown that the pattern-based approach can lead to interactive exhibits creating a more intuitive, effective, and enjoyable user experience, which captures some of the characteristics of Alexander's *Quality Without a Name.*

6.3   Further Research

Extending and refining languages

The obvious next steps are to refine and extend the existing pattern languages, particularly the HCI pattern language for interactive exhibits. Several patterns could use additional successful examples and more pieces of empirical evidence, and new patterns can easily extend these languages in many directions.

It would also be interesting to apply the pattern principle of this text to another entirely different application domain, in order to underline the general validity of this approach. As outlined in the approach, that domain has to show some aspects of a problem-solving or "designing" activity to be feasible for this approach. It has to be pointed out, however, that the pattern approach has in fact already been applied to a multiplicity of new domains, as indicated in the survey in chapter 2.

New application
domains

Another obvious next step is to refine the design of PET, and implement a more complete authoring environment for working with pattern languages in the format defined by this work. Such a support system could help authors to structure their writing process more easily, and it could help readers to create various views onto the pattern data, according to their own needs and preferences regarding subject area, detail, format, and presentation. In an effort stemming from the CHI 2000 workshop, we are currently looking at an improved XML definition of patterns that is based on the formal definition presented in chapter 3.

Computer support

Finally, at a patterns workshop of the British HCI Group in London in November 2000, participants have formed a Task Group for HCI Design Patterns, lead by the author, within the International Federation of Information Processing (IFIP). This offers organizational and financial support for future activities, such as HCI pattern writers' workshops, collaborative publication efforts, an online journal, or a networked repository of peer-reviewed HCI patterns.

BHCI 2000
Workshop: IFIP Task
Group

In recent years, the field of HCI design patterns has gained momentum, and it appears that this format is now beginning to gain acceptance within the HCI community. This work will be the first book publication on this exciting subject, and it will be interesting to see in what ways the field adopts and builds upon the ideas presented here.

Bibliography

ACM SIGCHI. *Curricula for Human–Computer Interaction.* ACM Press, New York, 1992.

Gregg Akkerman. Professional keyboard studies, 2000. http://members.aol.com/gakkerman/index.htm.

Lauralee Alben, Jim Faris, and Harry Sadler. Making it Macintosh: Designing the message when the message is design. *Interactions*, **1**(1):10–20, January 1994.

Christopher Alexander. *The Timeless Way of Building.* Oxford University Press, 1979.

Christopher Alexander. Keynote Speech, OOPSLA'96 11th Annual ACM Conference on Object-Oriented Programming Systems, Languages and Applications (October 6-10, 1996, San Jose, California), 1996. (Conference video).

Christopher Alexander, Sara Ishikawa, Murray Silverstein, Max Jacobson, Ingrid Fiksdahl-King, and Shlomo Angel. *A Pattern Language: Towns, Buildings, Construction.* Oxford University Press, 1977.

Christopher Alexander, Murray Silverstein, Shlomo Angel, Sara Ishikawa, and Denny Abrams. *The Oregon Experiment.* Oxford University Press, 1988.

Apple Computer. *Macintosh Human Interface Guidelines.* Addison-Wesley, Reading, MA, 1992.

Lon Barfield, Willie van Burgsteden, Ruud Lanfermeijer, Bert Mulder, Jurriënne Ossewold, Dick Rijken, and

Philippe Wegner. Interaction design at the Utrecht School of the Arts. *SIGCHI Bulletin*, **26**(3):49–79, 1994.

Lawrence W. Barsalou. *Cognitive Psychology: An Overview for Cognitive Scientists*. Tutorial Essays in Cognitive Science. Lawrence Erlbaum Associates, Hillsdale, NJ, 1992.

Elisabeth Bayle, Rachel Bellamy, George Casaday, Thomas Erickson, Sally Fincher, Beki Grinter, Ben Gross, Diane Lehder, Hans Marmolin, Brian Moore, Colin Potts, Grant Skousen, and John Thomas. Putting it all together: Towards a pattern language for interaction design. *SIGCHI Bulletin*, **30**(1):17–23, January 1998.

Kent Beck and Ward Cunningham. Using pattern languages for object-oriented programs. Technical Report CR-87-43, Tektronix, Inc., September 17, 1987. Presented at the OOPSLA'87 workshop on Specification and Design for Object-Oriented Programming.

Joachim-Ernst Berendt, editor. *Die Story des Jazz. Vom New Orleans zum Rock Jazz*. Reinbek, Hamburg, 1978.

Bernhard Binkowski, editor. *Musik Um Uns*. J. B. Metzler, Stuttgart, 1988.

Jan Borchers, Oliver Deussen, and Clemens Knörzer. Getting it across: Layout issues for kiosk systems. *Proceedings of the Workshop on W3-Based Online Kiosk Systems, WWW'95 Third International World-Wide Web Conference*, Darmstadt, 1995. Reprinted in *SIGCHI Bulletin*, **27**(4):68–74, October 1995.

Jan Borchers, Oliver Deussen, Arnold Klingert, and Clemens Knörzer. Layout rules for graphical web documents. *Computers & Graphics* **20**(3):415–426, May–June 1996.

Jan O. Borchers. WorldBeat: Designing a baton-based interface for an interactive music exhibit. In *Proceedings of the CHI 97 Conference on Human Factors in Computing Systems (Atlanta, GA, USA, March 22–27, 1997)*, pages 131–138, ACM, New York, 1997.

Jan Borchers and Max Mühlhäuser. Design patterns for interactive musical systems. *IEEE Multimedia*, **5**(3):36–46, July–September 1998.

Jan O. Borchers. Designing interactive music systems: A pattern approach. In *Human–Computer Interaction: Ergonomics and User Interfaces. Volume I of the Proceedings of the HCI International '99 8th International Conference on Human–Computer Interaction (Munich, Germany, August 22–27, 1999)*, pages 276–280. Lawrence Erlbaum Associates, London, 1999.

Jan O. Borchers. CHI meets PLoP: An interaction patterns workshop (at ChiliPLoP'99 Conference on Pattern Languages of Programming, Wickenburg, AZ, March 16–19, 1999). *SIGCHI Bulletin*, **32**(1):9–12, January 2000a.

Jan O. Borchers. A pattern approach to interaction design. In *Proceedings of the ACM DIS 2000 International Conference on Designing Interactive Systems (New York, August 17–19, 2000)*, pages 369–378. ACM Press, New York, 2000b. To be reprinted in *Communication In Design*, special issue of *AI & Society International Journal of Human-Centred Systems and Machine Intelligence*, Springer-Verlag, London, 2001.

Jan O. Borchers, Sally Fincher, Richard N. Griffiths, Lyn Pemberton, and Elke Siemon. Usability pattern language: Creating a community. Report of workshop at *INTERACT'99* (Edinburgh, Scotland, August 30–31, 1999); to be published.

Jan O. Borchers, Richard N. Griffiths, Lyn Pemberton, and Adam Stork. Pattern languages for interaction design: Building momentum. Report of workshop at CHI 2000 (The Hague, Netherlands, April 2–3, 2000); to be published.

Mark Bradac and Becky Fletcher. *A Pattern Language for Developing Form Style Windows*, chapter 19, in Martin et al. [1998].

George Casaday. Notes on a pattern language for interactive usability. In *Proceedings of the CHI 97 Conference on Human Factors in Computing Systems (Atlanta, GA, USA, March 22–27, 1997), Extended Abstracts*, pages 289–290, ACM, New York, 1997.

Alphonse Chapanis. The business case for human factors in informatics. In Brian Shackel and Simon Richardson, editors, *Human Factors for Informatics Usability*, pages 39–71. Cambridge University Press, 1991.

James O. Coplien and Douglas C. Schmidt, editors. *Pattern Languages of Program Design*, volume 1 of *Software Patterns Series*. Addison-Wesley, Reading, MA, 1995.

Matthias Dannenberg. Die Interaktive Fuge: Ein Pattern-basiertes Musikexponat. Master's thesis, University of Ulm (Diplomarbeit), 1999.

Peter Denning and Pamela Dargan. Action-centered design. In Winograd [1996], chapter 6, pages 105–119.

Alan J. Dix, Janet E. Finlay, Gregory D. Abowd, and Russell Beale. *Human–Computer Interaction*, 2nd edition. Prentice-Hall Europe, London, 1998.

J. C. Dobrian. *MAX Reference Manual*. Opcode Systems Inc., Palo Alto, CA, 1995.

Thomas Erickson. Interaction pattern languages: A *lingua franca* for interaction design? *UPA'98 Usability Professionals' Association Conference (invited talk)*, Washington, DC, June 24, 1998. http://www.upassoc.org/html/download/patterns.ppt.

Richard E. Fairley. *Software Engineering Concepts*. McGraw-Hill, New York, 1985.

Sidney Fels, Kazushi Nishimoto, and Kenji Mase. Musikalscope: A graphical musical insrument. In *Proceedings of the International Conference on Multimedia Computing and Systems ICMCS'97 (Ottawa, Ontario, June 3–6 1997)*, pages 55–62, IEEE Computer Society, 1997.

Erich Gamma, Richard Helm, Ralph Johnson, and John Vlissides. *Design Patterns: Elements of Reusable Object-Oriented Software*. Addison-Wesley, Reading, MA, 1995.

John D. Gould, Stephen J. Boies, and Jacob Ukelson. How to design usable systems. In Helander et al. [1997], chapter 10, 1997.

Åsa Granlund and Daniel Lafrenière. A pattern-supported approach to the user interface design process. Workshop report, UPA'99 Usability Professionals' Association Conference (Scottsdale, AZ, June 29–July 2, 1999), http://www.gespro.com/lafrenid/Workshop_Report.pdf, 1999a.

Åsa Granlund and Daniel Lafrenière. PSA: A pattern-supported approach to the user interface design process. Position paper for the UPA'99 Usability Professionals' Association Conference (Scottsdale, AZ, June 29–July 2, 1999), 1999b.

Stephan de Haas. Softwarearchitektur?! Ein Vergleich mit dem Bauwesen. *OBJEKTspektrum*, **6**:60–70, 1999.

Neil Harrison, Brian Foote, and Hans Rohnert, editors. *Pattern Languages of Program Design 4*. Software Patterns Series. Addison-Wesley, Reading, MA, 1999.

Martin G. Helander, Thomas K. Landauer, and Prasad V. Prabhu, editors. *Handbook of Human–Computer Interaction*. Elsevier Science, Amsterdam, 1997.

International MIDI Association. MIDI 1.0 detailed specification, document version 4.1. Technical report, IMA, Los Angeles, 1989.

Hiroshi Ishii and Brygg Ullmer. Tangible bits: Towards seamless interfaces between people, bits and atoms. In *Proceedings of the CHI 97 Conference on Human Factors in Computing Systems* (Atlanta, GA, USA, March 22–27, 1997), pages 234–241, ACM, New York, 1997.

Michael Jacobs. *All That Jazz*. Reclam, Stuttgart, 1996.

S. Janko, H. Leopoldseder, and G. Stocker. *Ars Electronica Center: Museum of the Future*. Ars Electronica Center, Linz, Austria, 1996.

Robin Jeffries, James R. Miller, Cathleen Wharton, and Kathy M. Uyeda. User interface evaluation in the real world: A comparison of four techniques. In *Proceedings of ACM CHI'91 Conference on Human Factors in Computing Systems*, Practical Design Methods, pages 119–124, 1991.

Scott Kim. Interdisciplinary cooperation. In Brenda Laurel, editor, *The Art of Human–Computer Interface Design*, pages 31–44. Addison-Wesley, Reading, MA, 1990.

Edmund T. Klemmer, editor. *Ergonomics: Harness the Power of Human Factors in Your Business*. Ablex, Norwood, NJ, 1989.

Wolfgang Köhler. *Gestalt Psychology*. G. Bell and Sons, London, 1930.

Wolfgang Köhler. *Gestalt Psychology: An Introduction to New Concepts in Modern Psychology*. Liveright, New York, reissue edition, 1992.

Thomas K. Landauer. *The Trouble with Computers: Usefulness, Usability, and Productivity*. MIT Press, Cambridge, MA, 1995.

M. Lee, G. Garnett, and D. Wessel. An adaptive conductor follower. In *Proceedings of the ICMC'92 International Computer Music Conference*. International Computer Music Association, San Francisco, 1992.

Robert C. Martin, Dirk Riehle, and Frank Buschmann, editors. *Pattern Languages of Program Design 3*, volume 3 of *Software Patterns Series*. Addison-Wesley, Reading, MA, 1998.

Gerard Meszaros and Jim Doble. A pattern language for pattern writing. In Martin et al. [1998].

George A. Miller. The magical number Seven, plus or minus two: Some limits on our capacity for processing information. *The Psychological Review*, **63**:81–97, 1956. http://www.well.com/user/smalin/miller.html.

Manfred Miller. Blues. In Berendt [1978], pages 41–61.

Max Mühlhäuser, Jan O. Borchers, Christian Falkowski, and Knut Manske. The Conference/Classroom of the Future: An interdisciplinary approach. In *Proceedings of the IFIP Conference on the International Office of the Future: Design Options and Solution Strategies (Tucson, AZ, April 9–11, 1996)*, pages 233–250. Chapman & Hall, London, 1996.

Michael J. Muller, Jean Hallewell Haslwanter, and Tom Dayton. Participatory practices in the software lifecycle. In Helander et al. [1997], chapter 11.

Brad A. Myers and Mary Beth Rosson. Survey on user interface programming. In *Proceedings of ACM CHI'92 Conference on Human Factors in Computing Systems*, Tools and Techniques, pages 195–202, 1992.

Marc Nanard, Jocelyne Nanard, and Paul Kahn. Pushing reuse in hypermedia design: Golden rules, design patterns and constructive templates. In *Proceedings of the Ninth ACM Conference on Hypertext*, Hypermedia Application Design, pages 11–20, 1998.

William M. Newman and Michael G. Lamming. *Interactive System Design*. Addison-Wesley, Wokingham, England, 1995.

Jakob Nielsen. *Usability Engineering*. Morgan Kaufmann, San Francisco, 1993.

Donald A. Norman. *The Psychology of Everyday Things*. Basic Books, New York, 1988.

Donald A. Norman and Stephen W. Draper. *User-Centered System Design: New Perspectives on Human–Computer Interaction*. Lawrence Erlbaum Associates, Hillsdale, NJ, 1986.

Open Software Foundation. *OSF/Motif Style Guide Release 1.2*. Prentice-Hall, 1992.

Steven Pemberton. Flags are not languages. *ACM SIGCHI Bulletin*, **30**(1):96, 1998.

R. Rich. Buchla Lightning II. *Electronic Musician*, **12**(8):118–124, August 1996.

Dirk Riehle and Heinz Züllighoven. *A Pattern Language for Tool Construction and Integration Based on the Tools and Materials Metaphor*, chapter 2. Volume 1 of Coplien and Schmidt [1995].

Gustavo Rossi, Alejandra Garrido, and Sergio Carvalho. *Design Patterns for Object-Oriented Hypermedia Applications*, chapter 11. Volume 2 of Vlissides et al. [1996].

Gustavo Rossi, Daniel Schwabe, and Alejandra Garrido. Design reuse in hypermedia applications development. In *Proceedings of the Eighth ACM Conference on Hypertext*, Hypertext Design, pages 57–66, 1997.

Daniel M. Russell and Mark Weiser. The future of integrated design of ubiquitous computing in combined real & virtual worlds. In *Proceedings of ACM CHI 98 Conference on Human Factors in Computing Systems (Summary)*, volume 2 of *Late Breaking Results: Suite: The Real and the Virtual: Integrating Architectural and Information Spaces*, pages 275–276, 1998.

Douglas Schuler and Aki Namioka, editors. *Participatory Design: Principles and Practices*. Lawrence Erlbaum Associates, Hillsdale, NJ, 1997.

Ben Shneiderman. *Designing the User Interface*, 3rd edition. Addison-Wesley, Reading, MA, 1998.

Norbert A. Streitz, Jörg Geißler, Torsten Holmer, Shin'ichi Konomi, Christian Müller-Tomfelde, Wolfgang Reischl, Petra Rexroth, Peter Seitz, and Ralf Steinmetz. i-LAND: An interactive landscape for creativity and innovation. In *Proceedings of the CHI 99 Conference on Human Factors in Computing Systems (Pittsburgh, PA, USA, May 15–20, 1999)*, pages 120–127. ACM, New York, 1999.

Bob Tedeschi. Good web site design can lead to healthy sales. *New York Times*, August 30, 1999.

Jenifer Tidwell. Interaction design patterns. PLoP'98 Conference on Pattern Languages of Programming, Illinois, extended version at www.mit.edu/~jtidwell/interaction_patterns.html, 1998.

Bruce Tognazzini. *TOG on Interface*. Addison-Wesley, Reading, MA, 1992.

John Underkoffler and Hiroshi Ishii. Urp: A luminous-tangible workbench for urban planning and design. In *Proceedings of the CHI 99 Conference on Human Factors in Computing Systems (Pittsburgh, PA, USA, May 15–20, 1999)*, pages 386–393, ACM, New York, 1999.

Martijn van Welie. A structure for usability based patterns. Pattern collection and position paper at the *CHI 2000 Workshop on Pattern Languages for Interaction Design: Building Momentum* (The Hague, The Netherlands), April 2000.

John M. Vlissides, James O. Coplien, and Norman L. Kerth, editors. *Pattern Languages of Program Design 2*, volume 2 of *Software Patterns Series*. Addison-Wesley, Reading, MA, 1996.

Terry Winograd, editor. *Bringing Design to Software*. Addison-Wesley, Reading, MA, 1996.

Polle T. Zellweger, Susan Harkness Regli, Jock D. Mackinlay, and Bay-Wei Chang. The impact of fluid documents on reading and browsing: An observational study. In *Proceedings of the CHI 2000 Conference on Human Factors in Computing Systems (The Hague, Netherlands, April 1–6, 2000)*, pages 249–256, ACM, New York, 2000.

Appendix A

Online Resources

This chapter contains the URLs of online resources that have been referenced in the text.

Borchers97   Jan O. Borchers: *actibits* Interactive Exhibits—*WorldBeat, Personal Orchestra, Virtual Vienna,* etc. (established 1997)
http://www.actibits.com/

Borchers99   Jan O. Borchers: The HCI Patterns Home Page (established 1999)
http://www.hcipatterns.org/

Erickson98   Thomas Erickson: Interaction Patterns Home Page (established February 1998)
http://www.pliant.org/personal/Tom_Erickson/InteractionPatterns.html

HDM00   Haus Der Musik Wien Betriebsges. mbH: HOUSE OF MUSIC VIENNA (HAUS DER MUSIK WIEN) (established 2000)
http://www.hdm.at/

Trætteberg00   Hallvard Trætteberg and Martijn Welie: Online HCI Patterns Writers' Workshop (established 2000)
http://bscw.gmd.de/

Appendix B

WorldBeat Sample Run

This storyboard-like sample interaction of a user with the *WorldBeat* interactive music exhibit conveys an impression of the system in use. The screenshots are reproduced at the end of this description.

B.1   *WorldBeat:* Interacting With Music

WorldBeat is an interactive computer-based exhibit about music. It was designed as a permanent exhibit for the *Ars Electronica Center*, a technology exhibition and venue centre in Linz, Austria. The system offers six *components* to let you interact with music in various ways.

B.2   Scenario: A Screen, And Two Batons

Walking up to the exhibit, all you see is a large wall-mounted colour display, a set of loudspeakers, and a pair of infrared batons hanging from the ceiling, as well as a microphone (see Fig. B.1). None of the typical ingredients of computer-based exhibits, such as computer, keyboard, or mouse, are visible—or, for that matter, of any relevance—to the visitor.

The entire exhibit is controlled using just the two infrared batons, a new, intuitive, and consistent form of interaction. The baton signals are received by a tracker below the display, and turned into navigation commands or musical input by the *WorldBeat* software. Like a light pointer, the right baton controls a cursor on screen. You can select objects on screen by pressing a button on the baton.

B.3   Start Page: Entering the Exhibit

Fig. B.2 shows the start page that you will find on screen when walking up to the exhibit (screen shots are in German, but are explained in the text). It briefly explains what the exhibit is about, how it works, and how to use the batons.

As soon as you have left this page by selecting the "Start" button, you know how to use the batons. There is, however, no critical information on this page that you would not be able to gain from watching somebody else using the system for a while, which makes it easy to take over the exhibit from a previous visitor.

B.4   Choosing From Six Components

The start page leads directly to the main selection page (see Fig. B.3). Here you can choose which *WorldBeat* component you would like to explore first. In the example screenshot, the visitor has moved the cursor over the *Virtual Baton* component; the icon fades into the background, and a brief description of the component appears. This avoid cluttering the screen with information, and at the same time offers some support with the selection without forcing you to enter the component by clicking on it. The "Back" button leads back to the start page.

Once you have decided which component to try, and clicked on its icon, you get to its respective start page. The next sections give brief examples of using each component.

B.5 *Virtual Baton:*
Conducting A Computer Orchestra

If you selected the *Virtual Baton* component as shown in the example, you first get a selection screen to choose between conducting a Bach minuet or Schubert's "The Trout".

If you select, for example, the Bach piece, you get to the page shown in Fig. B.4. As all component start pages, it follows the layout of the overall start page, explaining briefly what to do here, how it works, and why this technology is of interest. After pressing the "Start" button, you can begin conducting the piece with the right baton, and the piece is played with tempo and volume following the speed and size of your conducting gestures. At any time, you can return to the previous selection screen via the "Back" button.

B.6 *Joy-Sticks:*
Playing Virtual Instruments

If you select the *Joy-Sticks* component, *WorldBeat* offers you a selection of around thirty instrument setups (see Fig. B.5). To help with the choice, the setups were grouped thematically, and, for short-time visitors, three especially popular setups were made available as "highlights" directly on this page.

Choosing a setup leads to a page explaining how to play the instruments in it. As an example, Fig. B.6 shows the *Rock Drums* page.

All help texts on these pages are designed to be incremental: after reading the first paragraph, impatient users can start playing immediately. If they are interested, they can then read on to learn about more advanced features of each setup in the following two paragraphs. The "Back" button leads back to the *Joy-Sticks* start page, or, for instruments chosen from within a group, back to the selection page of that group.

B.7   *Musical Memory:* **Recognizing Instruments By Their Sound**

This component shows you a playing field with cards (see Fig. B.7). You choose a card on the left-hand side, play the sound that is "stored" on it by hitting with the baton, then select the right-hand card with the matching instrument name and picture. Choosing two matching cards removes them with a fanfare sound, and you score two points. Wrong selections make you lose one point.

After completing the first round, you can continue playing two more and increasingly difficult rounds with rhythm and exotic instruments, or you can finish the game at any time by going "Back" to the main WorldBeat selection screen. The high score remains stored as an incentive for other visitors, but is reset each day to give new users a chance to beat it.

B.8   *Query By Humming:* **Finding Songs By Singing Them**

This component, after the usual start page explaining the component and the songs available in the database, leads to a page initially only offering symbols to record a melody. You press the on-screen "Record" button, take the microphone available at the exhibit, and hum a short melody into it, then press the "Stop" button. The system then searches its database for this melody, and lists those pieces that best matched your query, together with their matching score (see Fig. B.8).

You can click on the piece you were looking for, and a digital recording of it is played back, which can be stopped at any time. After that, you can listen to a different piece from the list, hum a new query, or return to the main *WorldBeat* selection page.

B.9 *Musical Design Patterns:*
Improvising Without Wrong Notes

Fig. B.9 shows the most successful *WorldBeat* component in use: In *Musical Design Patterns*, you can first start an accompanying blues band by pressing "Play". The left-hand buttons under "Harmony" offer a selection of harmonic chord progressions of varying complexity.

Under "Rhythm", you can select how large the scale of the bass player should be, or whether he should use a standard walking bass pattern.

Below that, you can set how strong the *groove,* the time-shifting that is typical for the swinging feeling in jazz, should be. Pressing the button on the right baton as usual shows a scale on which the groove can be set to anything between a strange early timing, via straight (march-like) and the typical triplet groove, to a very laid-back rhythmic feeling. The tempo of the band can be adjusted in a similar way.

Finally, the right-hand buttons under "Melody" let you select how much the computer should help you with your improvising by correcting wrong notes. You can also choose from a variety of solo instrument sounds.

Once you have set the accompaniment to your liking, one of the most fascinating features of *WorldBeat* is available: you can improvise to the blues music, using your batons to play like on an invisible vibraphone in front of you— but without playing incorrectly. The system makes sure that your input matches the current harmonic context, following the standard rules of blues harmonic theory. Advanced players can switch this support off for a complete chromatic-scale keyboard with full creative freedom, but also full responsibility for wrong notes.

You can stop the accompaniment at any time to change settings, or read the online help that is available, as with all components, via the question mark, without music playing.

The "Back" button takes you back to the main *WorldBeat* selection screen.

B.10 *NetMusic:* Musical Cooperation Over Distance

The *NetMusic* start page explains how this components lets you play together with users at other *WorldBeat* stations around the world over the Internet. Since the laws of physics prohibit real-time collaborative playing over such distances, *NetMusic* offers a different way of real-time musical collaboration: you play one chorus in one voice of a piece locally, which is then broadcast to the other participants who can play their own voices to it and broadcast them in return. In this way, a piece is created by distributed musical collaboration.

Fig. B.10 shows the main *NetMusic* screen where you can select which part of a piece to play next, or to listen to the entire composition. Improvisation is supported for each voice, depending on the instrument. For example, a saxophone solo is actually hummed into the computer, where it is matched with the current harmony, and then played back with a saxophone sound. Other instruments use the batons in appropriate ways to enter musical data. Collaboration can range from spontaneous improvisation to long-term composition projects, since past compositions are stored at each site.

B.11 Leaving the Exhibit

You can leave the *WorldBeat* exhibit at any time. An integrated timer in the *WorldBeat* software resets the system to its start page after an adjustable amount of time, so later visitors will find the exhibit in its initial state.

Figure B.1: A visitor at the *WorldBeat* exhibit in the Ars Electronica Center.

Figure B.2: The start page of the *WorldBeat* exhibit informs visitors only briefly, so they can start becoming active themselves immediately.

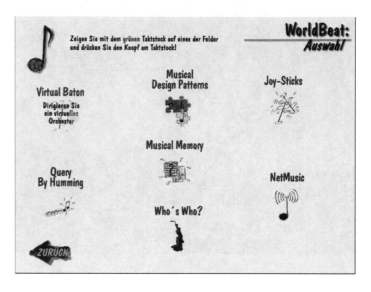

Figure B.3: The main menu page offers an overview and access to the various components of *WorldBeat*.

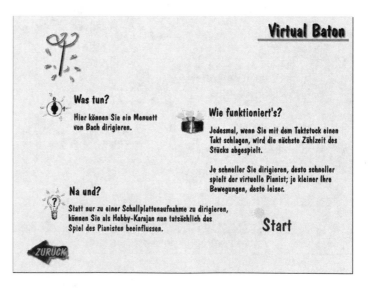

Figure B.4: The *Virtual Baton* page explains how to conduct a piece played by the computer.

Figure B.5: The *Joy-Sticks* start page offers various instrument groups, as well as a few selected "highlights" to choose from.

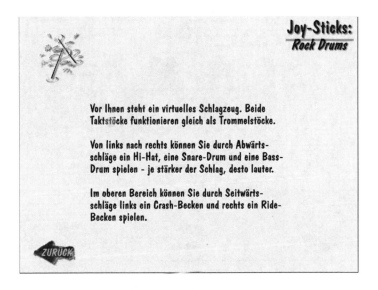

Figure B.6: The *Rock Drums* setup of the *Joy-Sticks* component lets visitors play a virtual drum set using the batons.

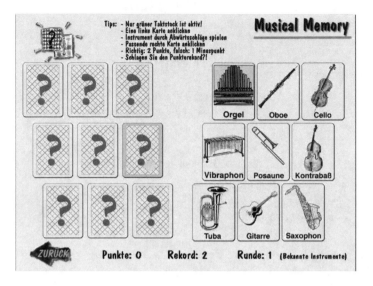

Figure B.7: *Musical Memory* is similar to the well-known card game, but with half of the cards containing sounds instead of pictures.

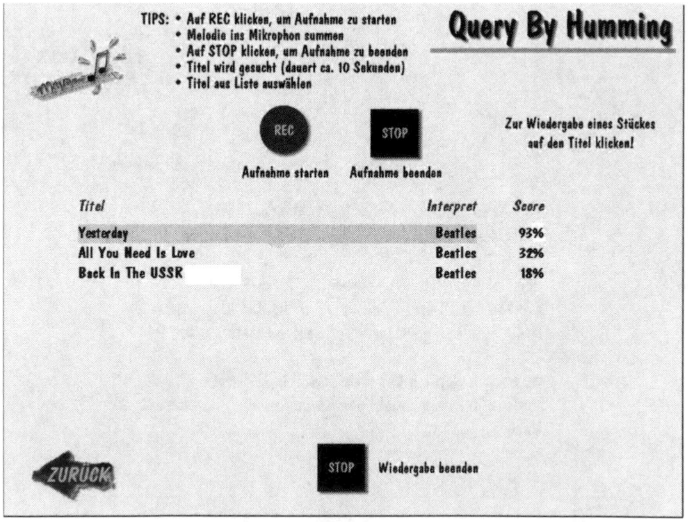

Figure B.8: In *Query By Humming*, the user has just hummed a query that returned three matches, and the user can now select the desired piece to listen to it.

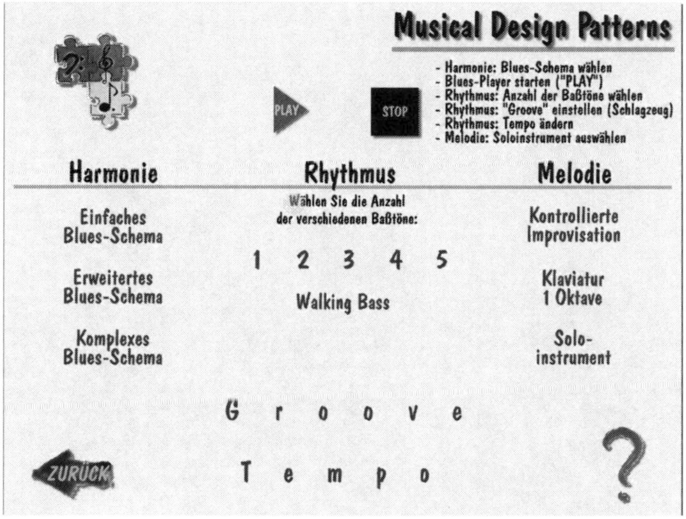

Figure B.9: The *Musical Design Patterns* component offers various ways of interacting with musical "patterns" of blues improvisation, including the ability to improvise to a band without playing wrong notes.

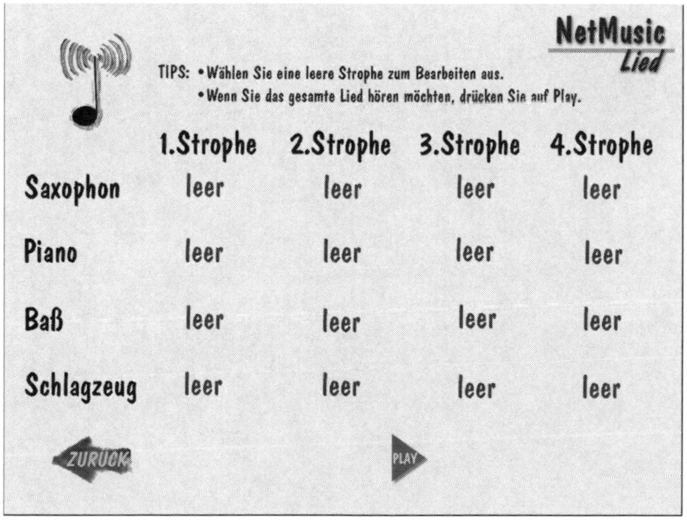

Figure B.10: The main *NetMusic* screen lets users choose which part of the collaborative composition to fill in next.

List of Figures and Credits

In addition, the author would like to thank Jenifer Tidwell and Richard N. Griffiths for their permission to use their pattern material on pages 34 and 42 respectively.

Unless stated otherwise, photographs and artwork in all figures were created by the author.

Index

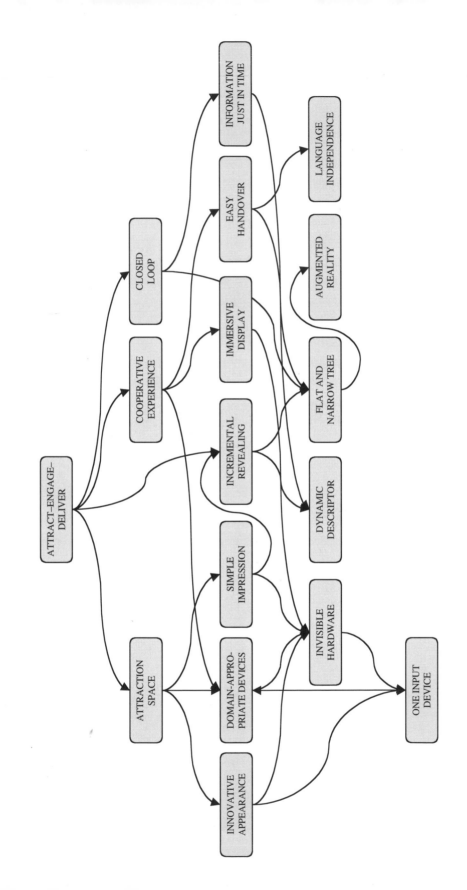